Passing

that

Interview

Passing
that
Interview

*Your step-by-step guide
to coming out on top*

JUDITH JOHNSTONE
5th edition

How To Books

First published by How To Books Ltd, 3 Newtec Place,
Magdalen Road, Oxford OX4 1RE. United Kingdom.
Tel: (01865) 793806. Fax: (01865) 248780.
email: info@howtobooks.co.uk
www.howtobooks.co.uk

British Library Cataloguing in Publication Data
A catalogue record for this book is available from
the British Library

Cover design by Shireen Nathoo Design
Cover image PhotoDisc

Produced for How To Books by Deer Park Productions
Typeset by PDQ Typesetting, Stoke-on-Trent, Staffs.
Printed and bound by Cromwell Press, Trowbridge, Wiltshire.

Preface
to the Fifth Edition

This book is written for those who need help with their interview presentation skills. In almost every area of employment 'restructuring', 'downsizing' and 'delayering' are becoming commonplace, affecting people who thought they had jobs for life, and an increasing number of women are returning to work after career breaks. As a result, more and more people are needing to learn or brush up old or forgotten interview skills as school-leavers and mature candidates alike seeking re-employment.

Becoming a successful candidate is no longer as simple as it was. When every candidate becomes the perfect clone of the one before, you need to have that 'extra special something', the magic ingredient to raise your chances above the rest.

This 'extra special something'—which often means the difference between success and failure—applies to all interview settings, whether you are job-hunting, seeking a coveted place at the college of your choice, or wanting to present a good case for financial backing when contemplating self-employment. This book will consider how you approach all three situations.

So what is this magic ingredient? Quite simply, it is *thorough* pre-interview preparation. The single most common complaint by interviewers is still the persistent lack of preparation by candidates. Many sit in the interview chair without any clear idea of why they are there; others have made no attempt to take advantage of valuable background data made available to them in brochures or factsheets they received with their application forms. Ill-prepared candidates waste everybody's time—including of course their own.

In an interview you are 'selling' yourself, a process you began when you submitted your application form or cv. It's no longer a matter of just needing the right qualifications or experience. Although these aspects will play their part, you now have to demonstrate you also have the skills and competencies being sought, as well as the enthusiasm, motivation and commitment to make a success of the job.

This book begins at the point where you receive the letter inviting you to interview and takes you step-by-step through the process.

This edition contains an entirely new chapter on what to expect if you are faced with aptitude tests or personality questionnaires as part of the interview process. These psychometric tests are increasingly being used by larger companies and organisations at all levels of recruitment from school-leaver to mature candidate. Tests of any sort can produce anxiety. Not knowing what to expect can only add to this – and can even damage your performance. At least by understanding why they are used and what they are designed to identify in a candidate you are better placed to feel more in control of the situation.

Judith Johnstone

Acknowledgments

I would like to thank the following for help with essential material for the first edition of this book and those who so willingly provided updated material for the subsequent editions when I requested it:

Members of the Careers Departments: Keswick School; Queen Katherine and Kirkbie Kendal Schools, Kendal; and The Lakes School, Windermere.

Personnel officers: ASDA Superstore, Kendal; National Westminster Bank, Preston Office; UCB Films plc, Wigton; East Cumbria Health Authority, Carlisle; and VSEL, Barrow-in-Furness; particularly Julie Dixon of Cumbria Personnel Services.

Members of the Careers Service staff at Workington and Kendal, Cumbria; and Career Analysts Ltd, London.

Staff at Charlotte Mason College of Education, Ambleside; Newton Rigg College, Penrith; Wray Castle College of Marine Electronics, Ambleside; and Lancaster University.

The telephone enquiry staff at Cumbria TEC and Windermere Jobcentre.

Alan Hurst and Ann Jones of the Prince's Youth Business Trust; Evelyn McDonald of the Prince's Scottish Youth Business Trust; and Richard Knowles and Brian Butcher of *Live*WIRE.

John O'Brien of Business Link Cumbria; Carol Dougan of the Glasgow Business Shop; Nicola Beynon of South Glamorgan TEC; and Mark Oliver of the Northern Ireland Development Board.

And finally Roy Davis of Saville & Holdsworth (UK) Ltd, Occupational Psychologists, for the wealth of material on personnel selection tests.

To everyone, many thanks.

J.J.

Contents

FENHAM & MASSEY LTD

Head Office
Fenham House, 27 Victoria Road
Chillingham CH3 9XQ

Telephone: (01234) 70707
Fax: (01234) 70717

My Ref: ET(T)/ED/357/PE/td
Your Ref:

This matter is being dealt with by:
Mrs P Edwards   **Ext:** 2439

16 December 199X

Dear Maxine

Appointment of Engineering Technician (Trainee)

Thank you for your recent application for the above post at our Martonby engineering site.

You are invited to attend for interview at the Engineering Divisional Offices, Massey Buildings, 23 Victoria Road, Chillingham on Thursday, 13 January 199X at 2.00 pm. Could you please arrange to bring with you all your educational certificates and report to the reception desk by the main entrance on your arrival.

You will be expected to sit a short problem-solving aptitude test at 2.00 pm immediately prior to your interview.

I would be grateful if you would contact Mrs Edwards at Head Office as soon as possible to confirm you will be able to attend.

Yours sincerely

W P Raine
Chief Personnel Officer

Miss M Roberts
46 Longworth Road
Martonby
Chillingham CH17 5RH

1

You Are Invited to Attend...

LOOKING AHEAD

Congratulations on overcoming the first hurdle of any job search—the selection process which decides who will, and who will not, be interviewed. This means you have already adopted the right approach—submitting an application which measures up to the high standard expected by your potential employer.

At this point it is worth reminding yourself that just as untidy or poorly prepared applications never stand a chance, neither do untidy or poorly prepared candidates.

The job search has to be tackled methodically. If you are applying for several jobs at once, you will already have found it useful to keep

- an **appointments diary**; and

- a simple **filing system** with each application placed in a separate folder containing copies of all relevant papers, eg advert, job description and a copy of your application.

Keeping a folder for each application is important. It not only prevents you getting your papers in a muddle, it also provides a safe place for your background material and work notes which are an essential part of pre-interview planning.

WHAT THE INVITATION MEANS

1. **The employer is interested**. This might seem like stating the obvious but it bears thinking about. The employer believes you have the right *potential* for the job. But –

2. **There will be other candidates**. A short list of three to five is not uncommon. Unless there is more than one vacancy on offer—which does not happen very often—the majority of candidates are going to be unsuccessful. You don't want to be one of them.

3. **You need to start your pre-interview planning**. This means not only brushing up on your personal presentation but also *researching into background information*, the area that is all too often ignored or not properly thought through.

WHAT THE INVITATION TELLS YOU

You can expect to find some, if not all, of the following information in your letter:

● basic information (time, date and place of interview);

● additional information (what you are expected to take with you and whether you will have to take some sort of test);

● who will interview you or meet you on arrival (not always supplied);

● how and when you are expected to confirm or decline attendance (by phone or in writing).

Existing commitments on the day of the interview

Right at the start you may see difficulties you need to sort out. The most obvious is when you realise you have existing commitments either on the day, or at the time, you are supposed to be sitting in the interview room. What should you do? Should you simply decline or explain your problem and ask for another date? There are four points you should think about:

1. Getting the right job is important
You may not get a second bite at this particular cherry. Cancelling an interview should be what you do as a last resort.

2. Interviewers don't interview all the time
They have other duties which may prevent them offering you alternative times or dates.

3. Interviewers do not always have the last say when it comes to filling job vacancies
Other senior staff might be pressing for the vacancy to be filled as soon as possible.

4. Being able to attend without causing any unnecessary ripples demonstrates your enthusiasm
As a general rule treat the interview as taking precedence over more commonplace events in life.

Sorting out difficulties as to interview arrangements
There are of course situations where the interview has to take second place. Interviewers accept this, such as

1. A death in the family where a close relative is involved
The emphasis is on *close*.

2. You will be out of the country on the date in question
Provided your absence is due to commitments which are unavoidable and impossible to rearrange, this is a valid reason. Holidays abroad, however, are rarely seen as belonging to this category.

3. You will be taking an examination for a nationally recognised qualification
This does not include a driving test which can be rearranged relatively easily.

4. You have a hospital appointment for urgent medical reasons
Non-urgent or routine visits, however, should be rearranged, as should non-urgent dental appointments or visits to your GP.

If you cannot attend for any of the above reasons, always ask if an alternative date can be arranged, although you may have to accept that this may not be possible.

In the unfortunate turn of events when two interviews are set for exactly the same time, you have to be prepared to decide which job is the one which appeals to you more. Most employers are not prepared to vary an interview date for the benefit of the opposition.

Time may be limited, so if you want to ask for a revised date, or ask for advice, you will need to use the phone rather than write a letter. If you are nervous about making telephone calls, particularly when it involves more than just simply confirming arrangements, make sure you are quite clear what you want to say *before* you start the call. The best way to do this is jot down a guide for yourself along the following lines:

- The phone number you want (and any extension referred to).

- The name of the person you want to speak to, ie the writer of the letter *or whoever is specifically named as the person to contact.* (This is important.)

- If you are calling long-distance from a pay-phone then say so. If there is any delay, ask if your contact could phone you back, or if this is impossible, when you should call again.

- Set out your problem *briefly.*

- If you are asking for the interview to be rearranged, have your appointments diary handy to check you are able to attend should alternative times and dates be suggested.

Make sure you have a plentiful supply of suitable coins if you have to use a pay-phone. This way you are not worrying about running out of change as well as trying to put together a coherent explanation for the call. Purchasing a phonecard may be a better option.

If there appear to be problems getting in touch with your contact person when you are using a pay-phone, for your own peace of mind ask to speak to a deputy, or anyone else who could give you a decision either immediately or if you called back later at an agreed time. Leaving messages with telephonists can be tricky. On a busy switchboard, messages can get lost or forgotten, and you have no way of knowing your message has not been passed on.

If you manage to negotiate a new date and time for your interview, make sure you note down the details on the original letter of invitation—and in your diary. You may not receive an up-date letter setting out the revised arrangements. If you have several interviews lined up in quick succession, it is all too easy to get into an unnecessary muddle.

As an additional safeguard when making phone calls, check you have heard the information correctly. Phone lines are often subject to interference or distracting background noises, so repeat any details and ask the person giving them to you to confirm they are correct.

Problems with the interview location
If you have applied to join a national company, for instance, you

may well be asked to attend for interview at a regional or district office a long way from home. If this is the case you need to be aware of precisely what is involved.

Travel arrangements
Check your route and work out how much time you need to allow for the journey with plenty of time to spare. This applies just as much to local as to long distance journeys. Remember, if you don't plan this part of your strategy properly, the rest of your pre-interview preparatory work will be wasted.
What do you need to know?

- Can you walk to the venue or not?
- Can a relative or friend give you a lift?
- Will you have to travel by train or bus?
- What is involved? Are there any changes?
- What costs are involved?
- Are there sufficient trains/buses to allow for a return journey the same day?
- Will you need to consider overnight accommodation?

Travel costs can be expensive. If you are faced with a long journey, check your letter of invitation to see if there is any mention of financial help to offset out-of-pocket expenses, for example:

- reimbursement of fares and/or
- allowances towards the cost of meals.

If the distance involved between your home address and interview is considerable, this should have been recognised by your potential employer. Your letter of invitation should therefore include details of suitable accommodation and the level of financial help available to meet the costs involved. If there is no mention of these, check what financial help is on offer, if any.
Follow the same telephone procedure recommended earlier—know who you want to speak to and what you want to say. Explain why you are phoning and note down on your letter any additional information you are given. Again make sure you speak to someone who is in a position to give you a straight answer.
It is especially advisable to repeat any financial details given to you over the phone to prevent misunderstandings. Any errors can then be put right immediately. You don't want to find yourself

having any hassle about your entitlement at some future date, particularly if you are going to be badly out of pocket.

What if no financial assistance is on offer?
This is a matter of personal judgement: if you have plenty of irons in the fire with several other interviews coming up, you may decide the expense is simply not worth it. Alternatively, you might want to move heaven and earth to have a crack at this particular job.

Don't neglect the possibility of asking your family or friends for support, either by direct funding or by providing accommodation if they live nearer the interview venue.

If you are unable to finance yourself and are unemployed, you may qualify for assistance under the Employment Service **Travel to Interview Scheme**. You can qualify if:

- you have been unemployed for 13 weeks and claiming benefit or National Insurance Credits (or if someone is claiming benefits on your behalf);

- you have been invited for a definite interview for a specific job;

- you have been living in your current area for at least 4 weeks;

- the interview must be in the UK and beyond normal daily travelling distance of your home area (30 miles); and

- the job must be for more than 30 hours a week, must not be seasonal, temporary or on a short-term fixed contract.

Different areas of the country have different travel to work patterns. Contact your Jobcentre for full details of the scheme as soon as you know you have an interview and check whether you qualify for help. If you do, you must make your application *before* you travel. The Jobcentre may have to confirm some information with your potential employer. This is normally done before the interview so that you will know in advance whether assistance can be given or not.

Disability or mobility problems
Getting a crack at the employment market is hard enough if you suffer from some form of disability. So it doesn't help when people who are able-bodied seem unaware of even the most basic problems you have to face every day.

The Disability Discrimination Act 1995 gives new rights to disabled people both in work and looking for work. 'Disability' is classed as being substantial and having a long-term effect, ie it is expected to last for 12 months. The disability can be physical, sensory or mental and includes severe disfigurement.

It is now against the law for an employer of 15 or more people to treat a disabled person less favourably than someone who is not disabled, unless there is a very good reason for doing so. Even employers with fewer than 15 employees will be encouraged to follow good practice guidelines. If the recruitment advert of your prospective employer contained the disability symbol 'Positive About Disabled People', you can be certain the employer has made five specific commitments:

- to interview all applicants with a disability who meet the minimum criteria for a job vacancy and consider them on their abilities;

- to ask disabled employees at least once a year what can be done to make sure they can develop and use their abilities at work;

- to make every effort when employees become disabled to ensure they stay in employment;

- to take action to ensure that key employees develop the awareness of disability needed to make these commitments work; and

- to review these commitments and what has been achieved every year, plan ways to improve them and let all employees know about progress and future plans.

If your disability is one of restricted mobility, you should have already made this clear in your original application. If you did not, you could be wasting everyone's time. Although the Act expects employers to make 'reasonable adjustments' to the workplace to accommodate someone with a disability, there may be genuine insurmountable difficulties, such as the relocation of heavy plant or equipment, which would make it impossible for you to work there.

If you have any concerns over how you will be accommodated, either in the workplace or during the interview, it is always better to check. The last thing you want is to arrive for interview faced with unexpected and unwelcome problems which can be both unnecessary and distressing.

Use the same telephone procedure suggested for rearranging the interview date. If necessary—such as with hearing difficulties—ask someone else to act on your behalf in your presence so that you are certain of the outcome.

Not all interviews take place in the workplace. Alternative venues such as regional or head offices often handle the recruitment and selection side of larger organisations. If you have any doubts about whether your particular need can be met, whether this involves car parking facilities, ramps, lifts or having someone on hand to greet you and guide you to the waiting area, for your own peace of mind check what is available. A caring employer will make every effort to provide whatever help you need. However, it would not be unreasonable of you to ask to bring along your own helper, particularly if your disability demanded assistance from someone who knew your exact requirements. So talk through your problem, and with luck it will be resolved. If it isn't, then it's better to know at once rather than later.

What should I take with me?

The letter might be quite specific in asking you to bring certain items, such as:

- school certificates
- record of achievement
- examples of artwork or technical drawings where appropriate.

Even if these are not specifically requested, it is a good idea to take them anyway. It shows you have used your initiative.

As a general rule, take with you anything which is *relevant* and which supports your application. Please note the word *relevant*. If you burden your interviewer with masses of unnecessary bits and pieces which do nothing to enhance your application, you may do your cause more harm than good.

Other things you might be asked to bring with you include:

- a pen (*not* felt-tip)
- a calculator.

Regardless of the situation, it is always best to have a pen (and paper) with you. It becomes absolutely vital, however, if you are expected to take some form of written test as part of your interview.

Neglecting to remember this most basic requirement will almost certainly tarnish your image, as well as putting you in the wrong frame of mind to settle quickly.

What if my interview involves tests?

You can expect to face a test of some sort when the job demands specific skills, such as an ability to handle delicate equipment or solve problems, or perhaps where you are required to have accuracy, speed or an ability to use figures. These are called **aptitude tests**.

Sometimes you will be expected to take a general intelligence test or one which is designed to highlight your **personality traits** or **motivational drives**, if these factors are considered important for the job. These tests are sometimes called **psychometric tests**. They have to be carried out by people who are properly qualified to adminster them, either **occupational psychologists** or **accredited users** who have reached the standards required by the **British Psychological Society** (BPS). Tests are often arranged at a different time and date from the interview. Sometimes they are even held at a different venue, so you have to be prepared to make the necessary arrangements to be able to attend these as well.

Your letter should tell you if your interview will include some form of test so that you are prepared for it. What it may not tell you, however, is precisely what the test involves or how long it will last.

Testing is being used by more and more employers as part of the selection process and Chapter 5 looks at what is involved in greater detail.

Any sort of testing situation is stressful. Combined with interview nerves, the effect can be traumatic. Don't get yourself into the position of sitting down to begin a test without knowing what to expect. In this situation you will simply find yourself unable to concentrate or give of your best.

If you are unsure about what to expect, don't hesitate to *ask well in advance*. Phone your contact person and write down any information you are given for reference purposes later. Be absolutely clear you understand what is going to be involved before you finish the call.

Who will the interviewer be?

If there is no mention of this in your invitation, make it your business to find out. It will help you to know:

● the name (or names, if more than one person is involved);

- their official title; and

- the position held within the organisation.

Why is this important?

- It tells you *how many people* you can expect to meet in the interview room so you are not taken aback by the unexpected.

- It gives you the *names* and *official titles* of your interviewers which can be memorised beforehand and used to good effect during the interview.

- It tells you *who they are*: your potential section or departmental head, **line manager** or personnel officer.

This last point is important. Knowing the organisational role of your interviewer, or interviewers, tells you something about the sort of questions they are likely to ask and what they are looking for in a candidate.

Section (or departmental heads) and line managers are interested in finding the most capable person for the job. They are practical people. They probably know everything there is to know about the job itself and will be looking for the candidate with:

- the right qualifications and/or experience;
- in the absence of these, other **transferable skills** which can be adapted easily to fit the job;
- a grasp of what the job involves (perhaps including technical jargon);
- visible enthusiasm; and
- the right personality and attitude.

On the other hand, a personnel officer is likely to be less concerned about the technical or practical side, leaving this aspect to departmental colleagues. He or she is far more likely to be interested in:

- your background (to give insight into your personality);
- what made you apply for the post;
- the way you see yourself developing in future;
- your possible career pattern; and
- what additional training you might need.

READY FOR ACTION

At this point you should have:

- all the necessary information to help you decide whether or not to accept the invitation; and
- a clearer picture of what the interview process will involve.

REPLYING TO THE INVITATION

Even if you are not specifically asked to confirm your attendance, make sure that you do so.

In the sample letter at the beginning of the chapter, the candidate is allowed to choose for herself whether to contact Mrs Edwards by phone or in writing. However, if you are given exact instructions as to the sort of reply expected, then *follow these precisely*. Don't risk losing 'Brownie points' before you start.

Confirming or declining the invitation by phone

Go through the routine discussed earlier in the chapter so that you are quite clear who you are phoning and what you want to say. Also consider the following:

- **Have you to phone at a certain time or before a specified date?**

- **Do you have details of the job vacancy to hand?** It may be one of several the person you are contacting is currently dealing with.

- **Are you mentally prepared for not getting through to your contact person?** In the absence of your contact, ask if you should call again and at what time, or leave a message with someone who is in a position to pass it to the appropriate person. (A secretary or personal assistant is a good bet.)

- **If you are declining the invitation, be prepared to have to give your reasons**. Make them good. Be brief and to the point. DON'T WAFFLE.

Confirming the invitation by letter

Whether you are accepting or declining the invitation, before you put pen to paper check the following:

- **Have you to address the letter to someone other than the writer?** If so, who? Remember if you address someone by name, you should close the letter 'Your sincerely'. 'Yours faithfully' is used for formal letters beginning 'Dear Sir' or 'Dear Madam'.

- **Is there a reference which you have been asked to quote on any correspondence?**

- **Has the letter to be received by a certain date?** If so, aim to reply *well before* the deadline.

Sketch out a rough draft—or several if necessary—and be completely satisfied with the result before producing the finished product. *Pay attention to detail* to show you have clearly understood the instructions you have been given.

Refer back to the sample letter at the beginning of the chapter and then look at the acceptance letter Maxine has written (page 23). What is wrong with it? See if you can do better by drafting your own reply and then compare this with Maxine's second attempt set out on page 24.

Declining the invitation by letter

If you have to decline the offer, keep it simple. Unlike declining by phone where you may be pressed into giving a reason for your decision, you do not need to state your reasons in a letter. However, adopt the same businesslike, methodical approach to your reply as you would if you were writing an acceptance. A suggested format is set out on page 25.

In all your dealings with potential employers, keep your standards high. You may find yourself applying for a job again with the same organisation at some time in the future.

CHECKLIST

1. Do you have to confirm/decline the invitation by a certain date?
2. Do you have to contact a named person?
3. Do you have to confirm/decline in writing or by phone?
4. Are there any problems over the date, time or place of interview?
5. Have you resolved these?
6. Are you likely to have to complete any tests at some stage during the interview? Are you clear about what will be involved?

7. Have you been asked to take any specific documentation or equipment with you? Would anything else be useful?
8. Do you know who will be interviewing you? Do you appreciate the significance of this information?
9. Have you mastered the use of the telephone to obtain and pass on essential information?
10. Are you confident you can compose an appropriate written reply in a businesslike manner?

46 Longworth Road
Martonby
Chillingham
CH17 5RH

Dear Mr Raine

Thank you for your letter.

I shall be able to attend the interview at 2.00 p.m. on 13 January.

Yours faithfully
Maxine Roberts

Your Ref:
ET(T)/ED/357/PE/ET

46 Longworth Road
Martonby
Chillingham
CH17 5RH

20 December 199X

For the attention of Mrs Edwards

Dear Mr Raine

Appointment of Engineering Technician (Trainee)

Thank you for your letter of 16 December inviting me to attend for interview.

I will be pleased to attend the Engineering Divisional Offices, Massey Buildings, on Thursday, 13 January 199X at 2.00 p.m., and will bring my educational certificates as requested.

Yours sincerely

Maxine Roberts (Miss)

Mr W. P. Raine
Chief Personnel Officer
Fenham & Massey Ltd
Fenham House
27 Victoria Road
Chillingham
CH3 9XQ

Your Ref:
    ET(T)/ED/357/PE/ed

46 Longworth Road
Martonby
Chillingham
CH17 5RH

20 December 199X

For the attention of Mrs Edwards

Dear Mr Raine

<u>Appointment of Engineering Technician (Trainee)</u>

Thank you for your letter of 16 December inviting me to attend for interview.

I am very sorry, but owing to unforeseen circumstances, I will not be able to take up your kind offer on this occasion.

Thank you however for considering my application.

Yours sincerely
    Maxine Roberts (Miss)

Mr W.P. Raine
Chief Personnel Officer
Fenham & Massey Ltd
Fenham House
27 Victoria Road
Chillingham
CH3 9XQ

2

Personal Presentation

LOOKING GOOD

If there is one time when first impressions count, this is undoubtedly when you go for interview. Most people involved with the selection of candidates admit to making up their minds about the person sitting in front of them within the first two minutes—in some cases even less.

There's not much point in complaining this is unfair: it's human nature to make snap judgements about other people for the flimsiest of reasons. Later on, when we get to know them better, we may change our minds.

Recruiters are human, too. The difficulty in their case is they only have a very limited time in which to get to know you. Their immediate reaction is therefore crucial.

If they like what they see, they are more liable to disregard other factors which might have counted against you. This is known as the **halo effect**. On the other hand, if you make a poor, or even bad impression right from the start, these same factors are almost certain to assume a greater importance—usually to your detriment. This is called the **cloven hoof effect**.

Personal presentation is all about looking good in the widest possible sense. How you look and behave tells your interviewer a great deal about your attitude, perhaps not only towards a particular job but work in general. Anything about you which sends a negative message is bad news.

GETTING IT RIGHT FROM HEAD TO TOE

Hair

No matter what type of job you are going for, your hair should *always* be clean and well-groomed. It simply doesn't pay to look scruffy. Wild styles and exotic colours should also be avoided. An interview is not the time or place to make a statement about your freedom to engage in self-expression, unless perhaps you are seeking employment in the artistic field.

Hair should never be allowed to obscure your eyes: it gives the impression you are trying to hide behind it, and prevents good visual contact between you and your interviewer which is vitally important. At the same time, make sure it is under control. Wrestling with a style which requires constant readjustment will not only irritate most interviewers but break your own concentration.

Beards and moustaches

He-man types please note. Rampant facial hair looks untidy, so both beards and moustaches should be well-trimmed and under control. Avoid cultivating a droopy Mexican moustache, as this tends to give an unintentionally gloomy, down-in-the-mouth appearance.

Regardless of what the current trend may be, take the trouble to shave.

Spectacles

If you wear spectacles, they inevitably affect your appearance. They should be clean, properly adjusted (so they don't sit on your nose at a ludicrous angle), and should not be broken or amateurishly mended with a piece of sellotape or fuse wire.

An interview is not the right place to wear sunglasses or the latest in mirror lenses. As with your hair, anything which prevents eye-to-eye contact with your interviewer should be avoided.

Teeth and mouth

Not everyone is blessed with a natural film-star smile, but regular dental checks should be part of your personal maintenance regime. So should daily brushing. You can't afford to be seen with the remnants of your last meal wedged visibly between your teeth.

Don't let bad breath ruin your chances.

Make-up

Remember you are going for an interview and not a night out on the town. Tone down over-bright colours and heavy eye-liners. What looks good in a disco can seem garish or even ghoulish in daylight.

Hands

Don't turn up with dirty or ragged finger nails. Even if your hobby sees you up to your elbows in machine oil, there are good proprietary brands of hand cleansers which, with the help of a nail brush, work wonders.

Ragged nails not only look unsightly, the sharp edges are tempting to fiddle with or pick at when you are under stress.

Clothes

In general, choose clothes that are neat, tidy, clean and well-fitting, and preferably made from fabrics which wear well and do not crease. Suits—both the male and female variety—are still expected by most interviewers, particularly if the job is to be office-based.

If you do not own a suit, choose clothes which you would wear to other formal occasions such as a wedding, or which could be described as 'smart casual'. Jeans and T-shirts do *not* come under this category.

Trousers for women are still not generally acceptable at interviews, so unless these form part of traditional ethnic dress, avoid them.

Also avoid wearing an outfit which is a combination of dark colours. This has the same gloomy, down-beat effect as a droopy moustache.

Shoes

Let these complement the rest of your outfit by being both clean and well-maintained. If you decide to buy a new pair for the occasion, wear these around the house to break them in beforehand. It can be hard to concentrate if half your mind is thinking how much your feet are hurting.

Outside weather wear

Be practical. You will need a coat or mackintosh and umbrella to keep you warm, dry or both. There is no point in going to a lot of trouble over your appearance only to turn up blue with cold or looking like a drowned rat.

Ensure your outer clothes are as immaculately clean as everything else, and preferably crease resistant.

Turning round

Don't forget the view from behind. Do you look as good from the back as you do from the front? Check this out in a full-length mirror. All sorts of things can let down personal appearance including:

- an untidy hairline, or a stray piece of hair sticking out
- loose threads from hems
- dropped or uneven hems
- scuffed heels
- labels sticking up at the collar
- twisted belts.

VISIBLE ACCESSORIES

Handbags
Avoid the outsized, lumpy, all-purpose bag that looks as though you are carrying a complete set of plumbing tools around with you.

Jewellery
It's best to keep jewellery to a minimum, simply because it can be distracting. Avoid anything that jangles or tinkles, including your good-luck charm bracelet, and steer clear of earrings that are flashy or bear a strong resemblance to a mini-mobile.

Other less obvious hazards include wearing badges, or symbols on chains around your neck, which have a religious, political or other possibly contentious meaning. Unless you have very strongly held principles about these, it would be wise to leave them at home, or in your pocket. You might unwittingly trigger a conscious or subconscious prejudice in your interviewer which could damage your chances of success.

Another pitfall is the digital watch which 'bleeps' on the hour. This is a distraction to be avoided at all costs.

Handkerchiefs
Apart from the situation where you are in the throes of a raging cold, have to hand a clean, fabric handkerchief for coping with sniffles or sneezes. Paper tissues are ideal for everyday use, but are apt to reduce themselves to messy shreds or a crumpled ball if pulled in and out of pockets too often.

INVISIBLE ACCESSORIES

Perfume and aftershave
As with jewellery, keep these to a minimum. You do not know whether you will be sharing a small, confined room with your interviewer. Under these circumstances your scent could be

overpowering, or worse still, set off an allergic reaction.

Some scents, combined with perspiration brought on by anxiety, can quickly deteriorate into unpleasantly stale odours.

Hairspray

Choose an unperfumed variety, particularly if you are already using a scented product of some description. Conflicting aromas can be just as nauseating as an over-abundance of one.

Body odour

Don't have it! Start the day with a bath or shower. Again, choose an unperfumed deodorant if you intend to use any other scented product.

YOUR PERSONAL ACTION PLAN

At this point, using what you have read so far as a guide, make a personal list of what action you need to take, and when, to ensure your own appearance will be up to scratch in time for your interview.

Make another list showing what clothes and accessories you intend to wear or take with you, including outdoor clothing. If you already have everything you need, check the items over to see if they need cleaning or altering in any way. Will you need to buy anything new? Try on the whole outfit. Are you satisfied with the total effect?

PLANNING TO STAY OVERNIGHT

As well as the items you need to take with you for the interview, you will also need:

- an overnight bag of appropriate size;
- night attire;
- a personal maintenance kit comprising soap, toothpaste, toothbrush, flannel, small towel, deodorant and shaver (if appropriate);
- brush/comb and hairspray (if appropriate);
- clean underwear;
- travel alarm clock; and
- any other essentials you might need eg medical supplies.

It's best to travel in different clothes from those you want to wear at the interview. This will protect your best outfit from becoming travel-weary or accidentally stained. As mentioned earlier in the chapter, crease-resistant interview clothes are a good choice in any case, but they are an absolute must if you have to pack them.

REHEARSALS FOR ACTING THE PART

Once you are satisfied with the way you look, it's time to consider the importance of the way you behave under stress, the role of positive body language, and clear speaking.

What will I need to think about?

There are four areas that deserve attention:

- nervous mannerisms
- irritating habits
- negative body language and bad posture
- poor speech in quality or content.

NERVOUS MANNERISMS AND IRRITATING HABITS

Mannerisms

Under stress it is sometimes difficult to hide how anxious you are and an interview is the ideal place to suffer from stress.

There are probably as many nervous mannerisms as there are people but the following are a cross-section of the most common. So ask yourself, if you are put on the spot, do you

- shuffle your shoulders or squirm in your seat?
- bite or chew your lips?
- toss your head repeatedly?
- twine your fingers around one another?
- tap the floor with your foot or 'bounce' the upper foot up and down after crossing your legs?
- scratch your cheek, ear, nose, chin or neck?

Irritating habits

These are very closely connected with nervous mannerisms and just as common. When you are thinking or listening under pressure, do you

- jingle spare change in your pocket?
- sniff repeatedly?
- pick at your nails?
- fiddle with a pen?
- fiddle with your jewellery?
- coil your hair round a finger?

You might of course be totally unaware of showing your anxiety so openly. The effect of exhibiting these stress patterns during an interview, however, is that at a very basic level you divert the attention of the interviewer from what you are saying to what you are doing, and in an extreme case you will generate impatience and irritability.

POSITIVE POSTURE AND BODY LANGUAGE

It's impossible to fake a positive attitude. However, adopting a positive approach to both your posture and the way you use your body during an interview can often instil a sense of well-being, and therefore a more positive and confident manner. Conversely, inattention to these aspects of your presentation can undermine everything else.

Here are some simple guidelines to help you make a good impression.

Entering the room

Do – walk forward confidently, body straight, head up.
– smile, and be prepared to shake hands briefly but positively if your interviewer offers to shake yours.

Don't – shamble in with hands in pockets, head down.
– burst into the room grinning inanely, extending your hand from the moment you are across the threshold.
– ignore a proffered hand.
– give a pump-handle handshake.
– give a wet-fish handshake.

Sitting down and settling in

Do – move the chair discreetly if you find yourself unable to sit

down without colliding with other furniture.
- sit straight, but in a relaxed, comfortable position which won't encourage you to shuffle around later on.
- keep your hands relaxed, preferably in your lap.
- maintain good **eye contact** with the interviewer as soon as you have settled.

Don't – hunch forward in your seat like a sack of potatoes.
- lean back nonchalantly with your legs outstretched in front of you.
- entwine your legs around those of the chair.
- sit on the edge of the seat.
- grip the arms of the chair (if there are any).
- cross your arms defensively in front of you.
- fix your eyes on the floor, or the wall behind the interviewer, when speaking.

GOOD SPEAKING

This is not about *what* you say, but *how* you say it. It has nothing to do with trying to mask a particularly strong dialect or accent, or overcoming a bad speech impediment such as stuttering—although making yourself understood has to have top priority. The emphasis here is on being heard by the interviewer. It is vitally important.

Do – pause and think about your answer before speaking.
- speak slightly slower than usual.
- speak clearly.
- choose the right tone and vocabulary to match the formality of the occasion.
- use a varying pitch to add interest and colour to your voice.

Don't – mumble.
- swear.
- rattle out streams of words like bullets from a sten-gun.
- use trendy phrases because you think this is clever.
- be pompous.
- obscure your words by putting your hand over or in front of your mouth.
- punctuate your answers with meaningless phrases and 'you knows'.

WAYS OF IMPROVING YOUR PERFORMANCE

Videos

Without doubt being videoed under mock interview conditions is an unbeatable learning experience. It has the advantage of adding sufficient stress to the situation to highlight areas of presentation which need working on, whether these are your overall appearance, manner, behaviour or speech patterns. Errors leap out at you.

Most schools and colleges have video equipment readily available these days; does yours? Members of the local business and professional community are often both willing and able to act as would-be interviewers. There is nothing to beat the realism of facing a stranger who is going to interrogate you.

Mock interviews

If you are unable to use video facilities, you will need to adopt a variety of tactics to compensate.

If you can, always take advantage of going through a mock interview. (The questionnaire at the end of the chapter can be used to assess your performance. It should be completed separately by both you and your interviewer and used for discussion purposes during a review session.)

How you see yourself, and how other people see you, can be quite a revelation.

In the absence of a formal mock interview, you can always ask friends or relatives to act as interviewers, but this is very much a second-best option. Friends and relatives may feel silly or embarrassed, and you might find yourself unable to adopt the right attitude because you know them too well. The other disadvantage of an interview under these circumstances is that it gives you very little guidance on the way you look, behave, or what you need to work on.

Develop your power of self-observation

Checking how you move or walk by using High Street shop windows has some value, but because you are actively looking for the effect, it will not show you how to perform on other occasions. You can however always consciously practise other ways of standing, walking and sitting in your everyday life, so that these become second-nature rather than something to be worked at all the time.

Similarly, when you are taking part in formal discussions, either during lessons or club activities, mentally step outside yourself and ask if you are demonstrating any bad habits or nervous mannerisms when the spotlight is on you. Once you recognise these, you can then make conscious efforts to work at overcoming or eradicating them. If you are unhappy about your speech presentation, use a tape recorder to identify areas that need attention, and practise improving these until you are satisfied with the result. One of the commonest problems is tonal quality. Many of us speak without realising how boring our voices sound, even when we have something really interesting to say. This can readily be demonstrated by listening and comparing the speech patterns of the average man- or woman-in-the-street with the presenter of a TV or radio programme.

CHECKLIST

1. Is your overall appearance smart and well-groomed?
2. Are you maintaining a regular personal maintenance routine?
3. Have you alternative travelling clothes if these are needed?
4. Have you a suitable overnight bag and toiletries available if needed?
5. What are your nervous mannerisms/bad habits? What are you doing to control these?
6. Does your standing/walking/sitting posture look good? If not, what can you do about it?
7. Can you be heard clearly when you speak? If not, how can you improve matters?
8. When you speak, what are you saying? How well are you saying it?

HOW DID I DO?

Put a ring around the description which has the closest fit and add any useful comments in the end column.

Comments

Entering the room

Dress	Correct	Acceptable	Inappropriate
Grooming	Good	Average	Poor
Expression	Friendly	Blank	Hostile

Meeting the interviewer

Posture	Good	Could do better	Bad
Manner	Confident	Neutral	Anxious/ Overconfident
Attitude	Attentive	Neutral	Apathetic

Getting down to business

Eye contact ..	Often	Occasional	None
Mannerisms ..	None	Some	Several
Speech	Clear	Could do better	Poor

First impressions (to be completed by interviewer)

....

....

....

3

Background Preparation

WHAT DO I NEED TO KNOW?

Apart from looking good at your interview, which will earn you a lot of Brownie points, you need to demonstrate you are *interested*, not only in the job on offer, but also in the firm or organisation which is offering it. To do this, you need to carry out research

- to obtain as much information as possible on the structure and products or services of the organisation;

- to find out where the job fits into the organisational set-up; and

- to discover as much as you can about the job itself.

WHY DO I NEED TO KNOW IT?

Lack of background preparation remains the single constant complaint by recruiters. It is an area which is consistently ignored or skimped by candidates of all ages, yet it is often the vital area which will decide who is, and who is not, successful.

What will my preparation tell the interviewer?

How much you are prepared to research gives your interviewer the opportunity of gauging the seriousness of your application as well as your level of commitment.

Some recruiters talk of candidates who turn up without the slightest idea about the size of the company, what products it makes, the number of its employees, its organisational structure or even what made them choose the company in preference to any other. Others say that too many candidates make very little effort to show why they should be considered the best person for the job. Both types of candidates showed quite plainly they had no real interest in either the company or the job in question. They had obviously given very little thought to their application beyond making themselves look good on paper. It is not surprising they were unsuccessful.

To repeat what was said in Chapter 1, being invited to interview does not mean the job will automatically be yours. There will be other candidates. You need to have that 'something' extra if you want to succeed.

What will my preparation do for me?

Thorough background preparation does three things:

- it boosts your confidence by making the interview that much easier to handle;

- it concentrates your mind on why you have applied for a particular job; and

- improves your chances of success.

The more you know about the products or services of an organisation, the better you will be able to talk about them, or ask questions.

Once you know the size and **organisational structure** of the company, you can put the job into better perspective. It may be part of a large division with plenty of opportunities for promotion, or it may be restricted to a small section with a broader base of activities. Finding out gives you the opportunity to ask intelligent questions.

Concentrating on what qualifications and skills the recruiter will be looking for also gives you the opportunity to spot those awkward grey areas in your application. This gives you plenty of time before your interview to consider how best to reduce their impact—by emphasising your stronger points. It also helps you identify aspects of the job which might need clarification before you decide to take it if it were offered to you.

GETTING TO KNOW THE ORGANISATION

There should be no real problem here because there are so many ways of putting together a comprehensive picture of your potential employer.

The job advert
This almost always includes a basic description of the employer such as 'a large multi-national organisation', 'expanding business', or 'local well-established family firm'.

Information sent to candidates
Larger organisations almost always send out factsheets, brochures or information packs to candidates. These are brimful of product details, type of service, the extent of company operations, organisational divisions, number of employees and so on. They are a mine of information for the person prepared to make the effort to dig it out.

Public Relations or Customer Service Departments
Are you dealing with a large employer? If so you will find these departments are always eager to help with enquiries, and will often be able to provide you with the latest company annual report.

Annual reports
These offer a useful insight into how an organisation likes to present itself to the outside world. They also contain details of the current trading position, future plans and other useful snippets.

The Kompass Register and Who Owns Whom
Both these tomes can be found in most reference libraries. The *Kompass Register* lists nearly 30,000 companies in the UK in four volumes. Volume III deals in basic details such as office hours, number of employees, product groups (which needs further research in Volumes I and II), application of products, sales offices, agents and subsidiary companies. Volume IV gives a breakdown of each company's financial performance.

If you want to know more about the organisation's international connections, check the *Who Owns Whom* volumes published by Dun and Bradstreet. These give you an insight not only into an organisation's UK subsidiaries but also its global activities.

Press reports
These can be particularly useful in providing news about both national and local companies.

Local careers service providers and Jobcentres
There is usually plenty of background information available from

these sources, particularly about local firms.

Personal contact with employees

Talking to someone already employed by the organisation will provide you with the nitty-gritty of everyday working life, and the less public face of the firm which you might be more familiar with from other sources—such as that provided by the PR Department or Annual Report.

There is the danger however of being over-influenced by an individual's perception of his or her workplace which might be distorted by personal circumstances or prejudices. Deal in facts rather than opinions and you will be on safer ground.

GETTING TO KNOW MORE ABOUT THE JOB

Here again, most medium to large scale concerns go out of their way to give as much information as possible about the job and where it fits into their organisation. Information can be gleaned from a variety of sources.

The advert

This is probably what attracted you to the job in the first place. The brief description of the duties and responsibilities attached to the post as well as the qualifications and skills needed will provide a useful framework on which to build.

The job description

With luck, you will have received this either with your application form or as a result of your written enquiry. If it is properly presented, it should tell you:

- the **job title** and the section or department it is attached to (if this is appropriate);
- the responsibilities of the job;
- the principle duties of the job; and
- the person or title of the person you will be accountable to.

Additional information, which might be on the job description or attached to it, can include some of all of the following:

- explanation of the organisation's departmental structure;

- conditions of employment; and
- training or promotional possibilities.

Conditions of employment

There are some very basic details about the job which it is essential you should know and understand. These are the **conditions of employment**. The details you need to know are:

- place of work;
- hours of work (specific times and days);
- rates of pay, allowances and bonuses;
- pension scheme;
- annual leave;
- sick pay; and
- period of notice to terminate employment.

All these points need clarifying, preferably before or during your interview, as they will form the basis of a binding **contract of employment** if the job is offered to you.

If it is unclear from any of the literature provided as to why the vacancy arose, or how long the previous post-holder held the job, keep both these points in mind to ask at interview. The answer, or lack of it, could tell you a great deal about the workings of the organisation at departmental level, and whether or not there are problems which would otherwise not have come to light.

THE JOB AND YOU

This is what the interview is all about. Your interviewers will be trying to match up the skills and personal qualities you can bring to the job with the level of competence the job requires.

What are they looking for?

Look again at the advert and job description. Make a list of all the requirements being asked for (or preferred) under the following headings:

- qualifications;
- experience;
- competencies (eg initiative, communication skills);
- personal qualities (eg cheerful, eager, outgoing);
- any special requirements (eg keyboard skills would be an advantage).

How do I match up?

You know from the fact you have been invited to interview, that you have something positive to offer your would-be employer. But is it enough? What you need to do next is compare your personal data with what is being asked for. You can do this by ticking off items under the above headings or by making a separate list for comparison purposes.

What if there are gaps in my background?

At this point you may find you don't have everything that is being asked for, or possibly what you do have seems a bit weak. Don't shrug this off as unimportant just because you have been offered an interview. Your recruiters will be looking for ways you can fill these gaps by other means, and you may well be closely questioned on these points. You want to be confident you can answer them.

The recruiters will be trying to identify **transferable skills**. These are skills which demonstrate your ability *in another way*. The following questions might help you spot yours. Make a note of any relevant answers.

- Have you any social activities, hobbies, or interests that demonstrate your capabilities?

- Have you held any key positions in school/college societies, teams etc which might be relevant?

Are there still any gaps?

If there are there could be two possible reasons:

- the missing factors are not crucial
- the interviewers will be looking at your potential to fill the gaps by one or all of the following:
  - willingness to train
  - the right personality
  - hard work
  - commitment and enthusiasm.

The second reason is more likely, and you could face some stiff questioning to discover if you have got what it takes. If you really want the job, you must be prepared to react positively and mean what you say. For instance, don't pretend you would be willing to study for additional qualifications at evening classes if you have no intention of doing so. You may be given the job on the strength of this answer and your future working relationship with your employers would be seriously jeopardised as a result.

SOME TYPICAL INTERVIEW QUESTIONS

'How do you see yourself? Why do you want the job?'

Such questions will form only part of your interview but are by far the most difficult. You will be asked to express *your personal opinion* and not simple verifiable facts. Waffle at this stage will only reveal that you have not thought through your application sufficiently; this is where a large number of candidates fail.

The questions which follow are the most commonly asked. But remember:

* Every interview is different. You may be asked all, some, or possibly none of them.

* The various answers listed are only suggestions to help you think out your own responses. They are not meant to be used as a matter of course or learnt parrot-fashion, something which should be avoided at all costs. If you learn answers off pat, even your own, they not only sound artificial, you may be tempted to make them fit similar but slightly differently phrased questions which require an entirely different reply.

As you go through the questions, write down the **key words** to remind you what you want to bring out in your answers and remember these. Don't be tempted into writing a short essay on each topic to learn off by heart—for the same reason.

What are your strengths?

Identify areas where you perform best and ask yourself how these could reinforce your suitability for the job.

What are your weaknesses?

Don't get yourself into difficulties by airing negative personality traits which might not easily be overcome, such as confessing to being over-critical or lazy. Instead, stick to minor factual problems which can be remedied by adding a positive rider to your answer. For instance: 'I suppose I didn't try hard enough at maths, *but I'm going to try and improve my grade this year at college.'*

How would you describe yourself?

Concentrate on the description of the person being sought by the original advert—eg enthusiastic, cheerful, resourceful or whatever. Try to put forward a picture of yourself which will match up to these as near as possible, and more besides. But you need to be honest, so don't go overboard or you will sound big-headed, self-opinionated, or even worse, false. By all means make the most of your good points but don't make them unbelievable. Qualifying some of your qualities may help. For instance, admitting to being *'usually cheerful'*, allows you to suffer from off-days like everyone else.

Why do you want to work for Widgets and Sprockets Ltd?

In other words, what attracted you to this company in preference to any other? Your answer must contain genuine, positive reasons backed up by supportive evidence, such as comparisons with competitors which showed Widgets and Sprockets to be a more attractive employer, or information from your research which implied Widgets and Sprockets would best suit your intended career pattern. Giving vague, unsupported reasons, or worse still, being unable to give any valid reasons at all, will tell your interviewer that, although you apparently want a job, you aren't really bothered about who you work for.

This approach might be acceptable if you are applying for a casual, part-time job, but if you are aiming for a permanent position with an established firm which has a pride in its product or service, your lack of interest in what it does will almost certainly make you one of the unsuccessful candidates.

Why do you want this job?

Your answer could well be one of the reasons listed below.

- I enjoy meeting the public.
- I like tackling a challenge.
- I think it might be interesting work.
- I like working with other people.
- I've always wanted to work with animals.

On their own, these statements lack credibility. They are quite meaningless unless you can back them up with something more substantial. For instance, can you give an *example* of some of the challenges you have tackled recently, or explain *why* you like working with other people, or *what* you mean by 'interesting work'? If you can't, then you haven't thought through your reasons carefully enough. You will be putting yourself in an embarrassing corner if your interviewer presses the point. Find genuine alternatives which you really can substantiate.

Look for examples in your out of school or college activities to help. For instance, your holiday job may have been at a supermarket checkout and you enjoyed meeting the customers. Your work experience placement in the High Street branch of a national bank may have fired your interest in financial institutions, or you may have had a particularly hobby for many years which has naturally led on to your choice of career.

If you can't make out a solid case for what attracted you to the job, then your interviewer will assume, probably quite rightly, that you are only going through the motions of job-hunting without giving the matter any serious thought.

What other questions could I be asked?

It should be stressed these are only possibilities, but they may help to keep your mind working along the right lines. Consider what answers you would give to the following.

- How did you get on with your school friends/teachers?

- What did you like most/least about your periods of work experience?

- What do you hope to be doing in five years' time?

- What do you think has been your greatest achievement?

- What is the greatest problem you have had to overcome?

- Who has been the greatest influence on your life and why?

- What book has most influenced your way of thinking?

Remember, in any answer, concentrate on the positive. This is not to say you should lie or hide a failing. If you have experienced difficulties then own up to them: show how you have overcome them or learnt from them, or how you intend to overcome them in future.

If you constantly dwell on the negative side of your life you will sell yourself short and prevent the more positive side from having a chance to succeed.

TO SUM UP

Never put yourself in the position at an interview of having to:
- lie
- blame someone else for a failure
- shrug your shoulders
- say you don't know
- say your best friend/parent/teacher etc said it was a good idea
- say you came for 'the money', even if this is true
- put yourself in a bad light without saying something positive to compensate.

Always show:
- you have valid reasons for your answers
- you are honest and open with your replies.

CHECKLIST

1. Do you have enough information about the firm/organisation? If not, how can you go about getting it?
2. Do you have enough information about the job? If not, how can you find out more?
3. Are there any gaps in your skills or qualifications compared with what the recruiters are looking for?
4. Can you compensate for these gaps and how?
5. What are your greatest strengths?
6. What are the major weaknesses you need to overcome?
7. Why do you want to work for this particular firm or organisation?
8. Why do you want this particular job?
9. Have you prepared a list of questions you want to ask at interview
   - about the organisation/company?
   - about the job?

4

Ready to Go

THE DAY BEFORE

By this time all your preparatory work should be complete. Last minute preparations should simply be a review of what you need to take with you and checking your travel arrangements.

The invitation letter

Re-read this carefully—have you overlooked something which might be important? Often in the initial excitement of receiving the letter, some key aspect of it can be overlooked or misinterpreted simply because the information was not immediately important when you drafted your reply. It may be the name of the person you have to ask for on arrival, or the scheduling of the test you are expected to take. Supplementary details such as this can throw you off balance at a critical moment if you don't recognise their importance at the time.

What should I take with me?

Apart from the letter itself:

- Have you gathered together all your educational certificates, records of achievement etc?

- Have you any additional *relevant* material (evidence of hobbies, projects and so on) which you intend to use in support of your application?

- Have you set aside writing or other equipment needed for test purposes?

- Have you prepared your queries and question sheet for reference during the interview?

Any documents, including your letter, should be kept flat in a suitable folder, preferably waterproof. Producing creased, sodden or mutilated pieces of papers during the interview is a downbeat image to avoid. But don't go overboard and buy an expensive executive case if this doesn't match the type of job you are trying for. There are plenty of alternatives available in any good stationers which won't cost a fortune.

Your overnight bag
Go through the list you drew up as part of your Action Plan in Chapter 2 and lay out the individual items to check them off at a glance.

Travel arrangements
Check these are still valid and that nothing has happened since you made your initial enquiries which might affect your journey. Have new timetables recently come in? Have the routes changed? If possible, book any tickets you need in advance to avoid a last minute rush.

If you live reasonably close to the interview location and have the time to spare, try out a dummy run to get the feel of the route. Even the simplest of journeys can be thrown into confusion by roadworks.

Additional items for emergencies
Although naturally you don't want to look on the black side, in an emergency, such as unforeseen travelling difficulties, have a plentiful supply of **loose change** to hand for urgent telephone calls. Write down relevant or important **phone numbers**, such as your contact person, or those of relatives or friends who might be meeting you, on a small card which can be kept either in your pocket or in your handbag.

Have a **comb and nail-file** somewhere about your person rather than packed away in an inaccessible place.

Put together an **emergency sewing kit** with a small safety pin as a useful extra.

If you are **accident prone**, a couple of elastoplasts and a supply of aspirins might also come in handy.

THE NIGHT BEFORE

This is the time to mentally and physically relax, confident that you have done everything possible to smooth the way to a successful interview the following day. Plan a timetable for yourself along the lines suggested below and stick to it.

Early evening

Pack your overnight bag if you need it
Don't leave this until the morning. It needs to be ready and waiting for you to pick it up as you go through the door on your way out.

Lay out clothes ready for the morning
Avoid having to scrabble around trying to find everything at the last minute. You want to reduce fluster and panic, not add to it.

Have a good soak in the bath
This combines your personal hygiene routine with the beneficial relaxing effects of submersion in warm water.

Mid-evening

Have a light supper
The emphasis should be on *light*. Avoid strong coffee or tea, which will tend to keep you awake, or anything which will over-stimulate your stomach juices which will already be quite active—probably more than you want them to be.

Run through your list of queries and answers to likely questions
Don't make a big thing of this by dwelling on each point. Read through them briefly with the aim of keeping the topics alive in our mind or refreshing yourself on an approach to a particular question.

Set your alarm for slightly earlier than usual
This is simply to make life easier if your interview is to be first thing in the morning. You want to have adequate time to get ready without constantly fretting over the passing minutes. You also want to give yourself additional time to pay an extra visit to the toilet. Nerves are bound to have an effect on your system, even if you are not conscious of feeling over-tense or anxious.

Have an early night
It goes without saying that you cannot possibly be at your best the following day if you cut down on sleep and reduce your ability to think clearly.

D-DAY

Setting off

There are some simple rules to help you get off to the right start.

Do – make time for a light meal before you go. Again, the emphasis is on *light*. Too much or too little food has the same result—tummy rumbles, usually to be heard when there is a definite lull in the conversation.

– check you have taken everything you need with you. This might sound obvious, but in the heat of the moment it's easy to forget something small, but important.

– wear a reliable watch. You really can't afford not to.

Don't – eat spicy foods. These not only play havoc with your system, they can also give you bad breath.

– choose indigestible foods. These can leave you with an uncomfortable pain in your chest, or even worse, produce uncontrollable hiccups.

– drink alcohol, take stimulants of any kind—or tranquillisers. Without exception, these will all have a negative effect on your performance, producing either misplaced over-confidence or muddled thinking. AVOID.

Arriving

Do – go straight to the interview venue. Unless you have more than an hour to spare, don't think of doing anything else. There is the danger of getting side-tracked or delayed in shops or cafés. Always aim to arrive with at least a quarter-of-an hour to spare and make yourself known to the receptionist. Bear in mind this person may be asked by the recruiter to give his or her impression of each candidate afterwards, so apart from being polite (which of course you always are), be confident and pleasant when you introduce yourself.

– be clear in your mind where you are expected to wait. Repeat any instructions you feel you need clarifying.

– find, or ask where the cloakrooms are. You will need to use the toilet and tidy up after your journey. This also gives you the chance to cope with other side effects of nerves such as cold, or clammy hands. A warm wash and thorough drying will help to control these.

- be polite and friendly to everyone you meet on the premises. You don't know whether any of them may have a crucial part to play in your recruitment.

Don't – arrive late or at the very last minute. You will make yourself flustered and unnecessarily anxious.

- neglect tidying yourself up when you arrive. Even if you feel good, give yourself a chance to check that you look good as well.

- be offhand or casual with existing employees who talk to you. Remember everyone could be a future colleague or boss.

Not arriving

This has to be the worst scenario for any candidate. The two most likely causes are:

- unexpected travel problems
- sickness on the day.

Unexpected travel problems

Strikes, breakdowns, roadworks and the like can all contrive to ruin your best laid plans. If you do find yourself unable to make the interview in time and you can get to a phone, you may be able to retrieve the situation. Make sure you take a pen and paper with you.

- Phone your contact person within the organisation, or leave a message with someone who can help you.

- Explain your problem briefly and concisely. Don't waffle.

- Seek advice and act on it, making sure you write down all the relevant details so that you can refer to them later. Relying on memory when under stress is *not* a good idea.

Sickness

Alas it does happen. If you are unfortunately struck down by the latest 'flu bug or anything else on the morning of the interview, act as soon as possible after the start of the working day to salvage something from the disaster.

- If you are unable to phone, ask someone reliable to make the call for you, giving them details of who to contact.

- Explain the problem briefly and concisely.

- Seek advice and make a written note of what is suggested.

In all cases where circumstances prevent you from attending the interview *never* neglect getting in touch to explain your absence for two very good reasons:

1. An alternative time or date might be offered to you so you could still be in with a chance.

2. You may want to apply for another job with the same organisation some time in the future. They won't look at you if you showed a lack of basic courtesy/initiative on a previous occasion.

Coping with a test

Even if you know well in advance precisely what your test involves, the experience will inevitably produce some stress. This will be heightened if you have never completed a similar test before.

If the test is being properly conducted, you should be told what it is intended to achieve. Written **aptitude tests** aimed at judging the extent of your skills and abilities have definite right/wrong answers. On the other hand, questionnaires devised to identify a particular **personality trait** or **motivational drive** do not, and are impossible to manipulate by attempting to guess which is the 'best' answer. You will waste precious time in trying to—so don't bother. Rather than working yourself into a lather, simply get on with the job in hand.

Do   – listen carefully to any instructions you are given.
     – note the time by which you are expected to have finished the test.

- read the questions *thoroughly* before starting. Too many errors are made simply through not paying sufficient attention to what is being asked.
- ask if you are unclear about what you are supposed to be doing. Don't waste time worrying in silence.

Don't – panic. This gets you nowhere.
- treat the test as though it doesn't matter. It could play a decisive role in deciding whether or not you are the right person for the job.

Waiting to be called

This is all about controlling stress. No matter how well-prepared you are, you are bound to feel tensed and apprehensive. This is quite natural. Faced with a challenging situation, the human body automatically reacts by pumping adrenalin around the blood stream. In more primitive times, this was to prepare people to fight or flee. But when you are sitting passively in a waiting area, there is a lot of super-charged energy swilling around inside you doing nothing. You need to consciously control this activity and channel it into sharpening your wits rather than dulling your senses.

Do   – concentrate on breathing with a regular steady rhythm rather than taking shallow gulps which tighten the diaphragm and stiffen you up.
- hold a handkerchief in your hands if you feel your palms beginning to go cold and clammy.
- mentally go through the points of your personal presentation you know need watching.
- look over your notes and questions, but only if you feel this will help you settle. It doesn't always—rather like last minute cramming before an exam—it can help or hinder.

Don't – smoke.
- chew gum.
- read anything which could divert your mind from concentrating on why you are there—such as a novel or general interest magazine. You are at an interview, not in a doctor's or dentist's waiting room.

Other candidates

Depending on the interview timetable, and whether or not tests have been set involving all the candidates at the same time, there may be others sitting in the waiting area with you. Different people react differently to this situation. Some welcome the opportunity to chat in order to relieve tension—or to pump information from others who have already been interviewed; others prefer to keep to themselves.

Under these circumstances, should you start up a conversation? Remember, it takes two. Even if you would like to chat on general topics to relieve your own nervousness, other candidates might not want to be drawn, either because they are trying to concentrate before going into interview, or because they think you are trying to winkle out useful information you can use to your own advantage.

Gauge the mood of the other candidates first. Their **body language** should help. Folded arms, crossed legs, eyes averted or immersed in reading something tells you not to intrude. A more relaxed sitting posture and willingness to smile on making **eye contact** indicates a greater openness. But don't go overboard and forget why you are there. You still need to keep yourself in readiness and third parties may find your casual chit-chat irritating. Always be considerate.

If you mistakenly encourage someone who is a compulsive talker and you really didn't want to get so involved, be polite, but show your mind is elsewhere by consulting your list of notes and questions even if you are not really taking these in. If he or she persists, despite your obvious signals that you would prefer to sit quietly, reduce your answers to simple short sentences or Yes/No where appropriate. In extreme cases, you may have to politely explain you would prefer to talk afterwards.

CHECKLIST

The day before

1. Is your background research and personal presentation up to scratch?

2. Are your travelling arrangements satisfactory?

3. Have you got all the things you need either packed or ready to take?

D-Day

1. Have you got everything with you?

2. Is your watch keeping good time?

3. Have you maintained a sensible eating and drinking programme before setting out?

4. Have you allowed sufficient time to tidy-up on arrival?

5. Who have you to ask for on arrival?

6. Are you mentally prepared for your test if you are having one?

7. Are you sufficiently aware of everyone you meet? Existing employees? Other candidates?

8. Are you making a conscious effort to relax?

9. Have you reminded yourself about particular points of personal presentation which need to be watched?

5

Selection Tests

WHY ARE TESTS USED?

The biggest single cost to any organisation is its staff. They are a very expensive item. If you have any doubt about this, just take a look at how much of the local authority education budget is spent on salaries. Organisations simply cannot afford to ignore the fact that finding the right person to fit the job is crucial. The wrong person can be a disaster, not just in terms of the damage they can do to the smooth running of a business, or the image of a company in the eyes of its customers, but also in the time, effort and cost of removing that person in a way which is acceptable in law.

Although the interview is still by far the most popular means of selection despite its subjectivity, the value of tests is that they provide a uniform set of standards to measure one candidate objectively against another. Good testing procedures undoubtedly take the pressure off interviewers and give them the opportunity to look at candidates from a different and completely independent perspective. The test has no axe to grind, no preconceived ideas, no prejudice: it simply records the information it is given and produces a result.

WHAT ARE PSYCHOMETRIC TESTS?

Psychometric tests, or psychological tests as they are sometimes known, include both

- **ability tests**, and
- **personality questionnaires**

but they are very different from each other in their approach and in what they are designed to measure.

Psychological tests have been around for a long time. Ability tests similar to those used today were developed almost a hundred years ago by a Frenchman, and personality questionnaires have been around almost as long. They were originally developed to identify men who would be unfit for the US Army in the First World War. Today they are used not just for selection and recruitment, but also to identify those with training or promotion potential. On the down side, they are also used to identify which employees should be considered for redundancy.

In the UK, such tests were originally used for selection by the Civil Service and the Armed Forces. However, by the early 1980s their use had expanded rapidly in both the **private** and **public** sector. Now you can meet them when applying to almost any larger organisation from local government to the larger retail stores, financial institutions and even temporary staffing agencies.

Psychometric tests are designed to measure your behaviour and what you are capable of doing both now and in the future. They can involve English and mathematical questions; intelligence tests; problem-solving; carrying out skilled tasks; questions on how you understand the world around you; your attitude to life; your preferences; and how you make judgements in a given set of circumstances. They can be pen and paper exercises, computer based or practical.

What is so attractive about the tests is their objectivity: there are standard methods for their administration and scoring so that any personal preference by the tester is removed completely. This is very important, and can be a useful counterbalance to any prejudices or subjectivity an interviewer might have which could work against you through no fault of your own. You can be confident too that the person carrying out the tests is either a qualified **occupational psychologist** or an **accredited user**, ie someone who has been specially trained to administer the tests. The **British Psychological Society** maintains very strict standards over who can become a tester, as well as over the standards and validity of the tests on offer from test suppliers.

Any employer using psychometric tests as part of the selection process should let you know what sort of test you will be taking and give you feedback at some stage afterwards, whether or not you get the job. Feedback is vital: it not only gives you some idea of how you coped with the ability tests, but also provides an objective snapshot of yourself as a person. This is particularly useful if you are not successful on this occasion because it helps you decide what sort of job you should be aiming for in the future.

Don't be frightened by the thought of psychometric tests. Think of them in a positive way as interesting experiences: they can throw light on aspects of your personality and ability you may never have appreciated before.

ABILITY TESTS

Ability tests are designed to show what skills you have. They demonstrate your abilities or **aptitudes**. The type of test you are given and whether it is basic or more demanding will depend entirely on the skills and standards necessary to identify the right person for the job.

What you need to remember is that with ability tests there are always right and wrong answers and there is usually a time limit in which you have to complete the questions. This time limit serves a useful purpose: it shows whether you work:

- quickly and accurately;
- quickly but inaccurately;
- slowly but accurately; or
- slowly and inaccurately.

Where accuracy counts for more than speed to meet the demands of the job, not finishing the test but maintaining a high level of accuracy might be more important than dashing through the questions and making lots of mistakes. **THINK ABOUT THIS.**

Types of test
Below are some simple examples to get your mind working. The answers are given at the end of the chapter.

Verbal reasoning
These tests examine how well you are able to understand ideas expressed in words. These can be simple multi-choice questions where you mark the answer which best fits the statement or idea in the question, such as:

Q.1 Dog is to Puppy, as Cat is to
(a) Mouse (b) Bitch (c) Kitten (d) Lion.

Most jobs involve the use of language, so this is one of the tests you are most likely to meet.

At a more demanding level, the test may involve several short passages each containing information on a different topic. After each passage there are a series of statements relating to the information provided. You are then asked to say whether each statement is true, untrue or unclear without further information. This type of test is most commonly used for graduate, professional and managerial recruitment where a higher level of analytical ability is needed than a basic understanding of the language.

Numerical reasoning
Here you show how well you are able to think with numbers and understand their relationship to one another. You may be given a series of numbers which are part of a pattern. They may be in ascending or descending order, or even a mixture of both. What you have to do is identify from several possible answers, the next number in the series. For example

Q.2 1 2 4 8 16   (a)24 (b)64 (c)48 (d)32

More complex tests are likely to include questions based on data contained in graphs or statistical tables which need to be analysed to identify the correct answer from several options offered.
Any job where you need to work with numbers in an analytical way, such as accountancy or auditing, is likely to attract this type of test.

Perceptual reasoning
In these tests you show how well you think in patterns and shapes. You will be given a series of shapes which are somehow connected to each other and you have to pick out the next in the series from the multi-choice answers provided. These can be quite simple patterns where you are asked to add two shapes together such as:

Q.3 [+] =   (a) [] (b)][(c) () (d) O

or much more complicated combinations where you are dealing with shapes shifting locations within shapes; clockwise or anti-clockwise rotations of the various components; additions or deletions from one shape to the next; black patterns on white backgrounds (or vice versa), and so on. You need a keen eye to spot what is happening from one shape to the next, and a keen mind to pick out which is the next shape in the series.
These tests have particular relevance to scientific work where the

ability to 'see' and think in an abstract way is a crucial part of the job.

Spatial reasoning
This is a variation on perceptual reasoning, but this time you have to think in three dimensions. The test usually comprises a variety of two-dimensional plans of three-dimensional objects. What you have to do is carry out the necessary mental maneouvres to pick out from the options provided what three-dimensional object (or objects) the plan will make. For example:

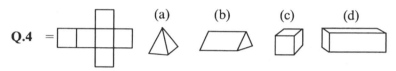

Complications arise when part of the plan is shaded or patterned, or when you are asked to take one three-dimensional representation away from another and pick out what shape would be left.

Spatial reasoning ability is essential for designers and draughtsmen, but is also a useful skill for photographers and hairdressers.

Mechanical or technical reasoning
These tests are only used to identify the technically minded. When completing them it helps to have a basic understanding of simple mechanics, but a logical step-by-step approach can demonstrate that even where you lack this type of knowledge, the ability to think through a process may show potential with the right sort of training.

The tests are multi-purpose and show:

* how well you understand written information;

* whether you can calculate quickly and accurately;

* whether you understand basic mechanics;

* if you have spatial awareness; and

* whether or not you can spot faults in a system.

They are invaluable in helping to select assembly workers, engineers or maintenance personnel.

Acuity tests

These tests are all about how accurate you are and how quickly you work. The time limit is usually quite demanding so that finishing all the questions is difficult. You may be asked to put several lists of names or words into alphabetical order, or check one list against another, or complete a series of basic calculations using mental arithmetic.

These tests help pick out the best candidates for jobs which involve, for example, filing, quality inspection or computer operating, or any other job where visual and mental speed and accuracy are highly prized.

Manual dexterity tests

These are usually very specific to a particular job and are designed to test the precise skills needed to do that job well. You can expect such tests if you are likely to be working with machinery where good hand/eye co-ordination is essential.

If you are applying for a job demanding keyboard or wordprocessing skills you are likely to be tested on your speed, accuracy and understanding of the technology involved.

CAN I IMPROVE MY ABILITY TEST PERFORMANCE?

The simple answer is—Yes. This is because ability tests are all about skills, and skills can be polished up.

If you are reasonably competent in something, practice will always make some improvement, no matter how small. This is not cheating, it is making sure you do not sell yourself short if you are capable of something better. This is not to say you would be able to sharpen your performance in all ability tests, but the chances are you could certainly improve both your verbal and numerical reasoning scores, and these are probably the two most important basic skills an employer will be looking for.

Ways of improving verbal reasoning

In some quarters, reading has gone out of fashion in favour of visual presentation. This is fine for some forms of learning, but the value of reading, even if this is from a screen, remains extremely important.

- **Read more**. Spend time reading the news, not just listening or watching it.

- **Read more carefully**. If you come across a word which is unfamiliar, don't just look it up, memorise its meaning as well.

- **Read more widely**. Don't limit yourself to one type of reading. Give yourself some variety. This way you will see how words are used in different settings and how the choice of vocabulary changes too.

- **Play word games**. Crosswords, wordsearches, anagrams—these are all ways to help you expand your understanding of the language, the way words are constructed, and when to use them.

- **Write more**. It may be good to talk but it does nothing for your spelling. Letters are still cheaper than phone calls. Keep a diary. Treat yourself to a Thesaurus as well as a Dictionary.

Ways of improving numerical reasoning

It's all too easy to reach for the calculator, even for the simplest of sums. But don't count on being allowed to use a calculator in a test.

- **Practise mental arithmetic.** Check bank statements, till rolls etc where the answer can be validated. Work out in advance the change you should get for a cash purchase when out shopping.

- **Buy a simple maths book.** Keep your mind alert to the simple arts of adding, subtracting, multiplying and dividing.

- **Study statistical tables and graphs**. If you are likely to meet more sophisticated numerical reasoning tests, absorbing financial reports, employment and population statistics and the like are a must.

PERSONALITY QUESTIONNAIRES

Personality questionnaires are not tests in the strict sense of the word. They reflect your *attitude*, the way you see the world and how you respond to it. They highlight your strengths and weaknesses as a person and what motivates you to do one thing rather than another. Because of this there are no definite 'right' or 'wrong' answers to the questions you are asked. What personality questionnaires bring out is whether you have the 'right' personality to suit the demands of the job on offer.

It has been proved that however much life's experiences shift and mould your attitude, how you function as a person tends to remain pretty much the same. For example, you will not suddenly become a fun-loving party-goer if you have always been a recluse. You may learn to enjoy social occasions more than you did, but the 'inner' you will still prefer your own company to that of others. It is this unique 'you' that an employer is interested in because this will affect how you use your other abilities.

ANSWERING A PERSONALITY QUESTIONNAIRE

What to expect

Personality questionnaires can be simple choice or multiple choice. They can be pen and paper exercises or computer based. Sometimes there are more than 100 questions for you to answer.

Simple choice questionnaires

These ask you simply to state a preference. For example:

I like someone else to take the lead   YES/NO

or to select one statement in preference to another. For example:

I like reading.
I enjoy tennis.

If you like both reading and tennis, you will find this task difficult, but the questionnaire puts you in the position of having to make a choice between them.

As you progress through the questionnaire, you will find the same two activities paired up with new choices. In this way the relative importance you place on a particular activity can be measured in relation to others.

Multiple choice questionnaires

These involve making a decision as to how much you agree or disagree with a particular statement. You are sometimes allowed to strongly disagree, disagree, be unsure, agree or strongly agree; or to agree, be uncertain, or disagree.

The wording of these tests is important because many of the statements are qualified. For example:

I *sometimes* make mistakes.
I am *easily* disappointed.

The words in italics in the above examples would not be highlighted in a questionnaire but you must take them into account when answering the questions. This is because you might agree you *sometimes* make mistakes, but disagree that you *often* make mistakes. Read the statements carefully.

Other types of questionnaire will ask you to say which of several statements most, and least, reflect the sort of person you are. Sometimes you are asked to give a simple Yes/No answer to individual statements.

Other variations include answering questions on how you believe other people see you as a person.

There is no time limit for completing a questionnaire, but you may be given some indication of how long it should take as a rough guideline. When completing a questionnaire:

- DO NOT agonise over each question. The best answers are those which are spontaneous because they reflect your immediate reaction.

- DO NOT be tempted to give the answer you think is expected. All personality questionnaires are devised to counteract this— some even pick out answers which are not true, or run counter to the general drift of the rest.

- DO NOT pick the easy option of choosing 'Unsure' or 'Uncertain' to avoid answering the majority of questions. You are selling yourself short if you do.

Personality questionnaires are interpreted according to specific, recognised characteristics, which is why it is so important that the person carrying out the tests is properly qualified. But although the tester 'interprets' your answers, this interpretation is in no way as subjective as it sounds: it is carried out using standard techniques which have been rigorously tested themselves over many years.

CAN I IMPROVE MY PERSONALITY QUESTIONNAIRE PERFORMANCE?

Not in the same way as you can with an ability test. But you can make every effort to familiarise yourself with the sort of test you are likely to encounter. The Further Reading section at the end of this book includes titles which deal specifically with selection tests and how to cope with them.

If you are given practice sheets to study beforehand, these will show you the type of questions you will be asked, and help to familiarise you with the layout. They will also give guidance on how you are expected to answer the questions. If you are not told in advance what is likely to be involved, do contact your prospective employer and ask to speak to whoever is organising the test procedure. Employers using psychometric tests responsibly are always keen to help candidates, particularly if it is their first experience of being tested in this way.

PREPARING FOR THE TEST DAY

Treat your test day as part of your interview. Re-read Chapter 4 on pre-interview preparation and apply the same personal preparation schedule to your test. Always arrive in good time and give yourself the chance to settle down mentally to the task before you.

THE IDEAL TEST LOCATION

In the past, tests have not always been administered as strictly as they are today. If you are taking written or computer based tests you can expect the room chosen for the candidates to be:

- in a quiet location away from any other distracting activities;
- properly heated and ventilated;
- well lit; and
- with sufficient personal space between candidates.

MANAGING THE TEST PROCEDURES

Before the test

The person responsible for administering the test will want to make you feel comfortable and give you the opportunity to settle quickly. Once they are satisfied everyone is present and suitably prepared, they will run through what the test involves. At this point you must CONCENTRATE.

- Listen to the instructions you are given.

- Check any equipment you have been given.

- Ask immediately if you are unsure about anything.

- Let the tester know if there is any disability which might prevent you from completing a timed test within the time limit, eg hand injury, difficulties with vision etc.

- Make maximum use of the sample questions you are given before the start of the test itself. Check how long it takes you to do them.

- Learn from any mistakes.

The test itself

With **personality questionnaires** there is less pressure. Your performance in **ability tests**, however, can be improved by polishing up test techniques.

- Quickly check the number of questions you have to answer within the time allocated.

- Mentally calculate how much time you can spend on each one.

- Work steadily through them at an even pace.

- Don't waste time on questions you can't answer immediately. Move on to the next and come back to the others if you have time later.

- OCCASIONALLY check your watch to see how you are keeping to your schedule. DO NOT keep on checking: this wastes time and interrupts your train of thought which wastes more time. Once or twice is enough.

- Ignore everyone else. CONCENTRATE.

Afterwards

The tester should let you know what part the tests will play in the selection process. You should also be told when you can expect to receive feedback on the results. This could either be verbal or written, but it may not be given to you automatically. If you have to actively make contact yourself always take up the offer.

In a quieter moment after the test, think over any problem areas you were aware of. See if there is any way you could make these less of a problem next time: sometimes it can be something as simple as a new pair of reading glasses.

CHECKLIST

Before the test
1. Do you know what type of test you will be expected to take?
2. Have you checked out what this type of test involves?
3. Are there any ways you could improve your test results? If so, how?
4. Have you arranged your personal schedule to get you to the test on time?
5. Are there any points you want to raise with the tester? If so, what are they?

After the test
1. Was there anything you were unsure of in the practice session?
2. Did you follow all the instructions you were given?
3. Did you use your time wisely in timed sessions? If not, why not?
4. Were you promised feedback? If so, when?
5. If you were given the chance to retake the tests, would you tackle them any differently? If so, how?

Answers to questions: Q. 1 (c), Q.2 (d), Q.3 (a), Q.4 (c).

6

The Ideal Interview

WHAT TO EXPECT

The Institute of Personnel and Development (IPD) sets standards of performance for professional people in the UK who work in the personnel, training and development field, or human resources as it is sometimes known. The Institute issues advice and guidance to its members on how recruitment practices should be carried out. It also publishes books for recruiters setting out good interview techniques to help them select the right candidate for the job. Because these standards have become recognised norms, there is a danger, when discussing what to expect during an interview, of giving the impression that certain circumstances and events will always take place. They won't. Not all recruiters are professionally trained personnel officers. As a result recruitment practices by many organisations may be less than perfect.

You should be prepared for your own interview experience to differ sharply from the 'ideal world' set out in this chapter. Your best course therefore is to use this chapter as a basic guide to plan your own part in a well-organised interview—and then study Chapter 7.

The interview location

A room separated from the hurly-burly of other activities is usually set aside for interview purposes.

Some recruiters prefer the more formal approach of sitting behind a table with the candidate's chair in front of them. Others prefer the less formal arrangement of easy chairs and low side tables.

During the interview, there should be no interruptions (except in cases of dire emergency), either from telephone calls or other members of staff. The good recruiter will have given clear instructions for any telephone calls to be diverted, and other members of staff will have been informed that the interview room is a no-go area.

The interviewer(s)

How many interviewers will there be?
You can expect one, two or possibly even three interviewers if the job you have applied for is fairly low-key. **Panel interviews** where there are more than three interviewers tend to be for more high-powered appointments, particularly in the **public sector**.

Who will do the interviewing?
The choice of interviewer varies from organisation to organisation; it may even vary between different departments or divisions within a single organisation. You may be interviewed by a personnel officer, a **line manager**, or even the departmental head—or a combination of all three. The interviewer is unlikely to be the same person who conducts your selection tests.

Will I be put at ease?
Regardless of how many interviewers there are, however, their manner should be friendly and relaxed so that a good rapport can be built up quickly between you. If they cannot put you at your ease within a short space of time, the interview process will be hampered by your anxiety—the last thing a good recruiter wants to happen. They will also want to show they are interested in you and what you have to offer, but at the same time will keep a tight rein on the interview timetable—so casual chat will be kept to a minimum.

What kind of questions will a good interviewer ask me?
Good recruiters use **open questions** (the who, what, when, where, how and why variety) to obtain as much information as possible in the time available. Although you may not see the immediate relevance of some of their questions—those dealing with your home and family perhaps—there will be valid reasons for these being asked to put your personal goals or achievements into some sort of context. But they will not pry into irrelevant aspects of your life which could not possibly have any bearing on whether or not you could do the job in question. Nor will they discriminate against you on any grounds whatsoever.

Will a good interview follow a set pattern?
Professional recruiters always work to a pre-planned programme. But this does not mean every interviewer will use the same pattern, or that interviews for roughly the same sort of job will be similar.

Far from it. The professional recruiter, however, will choose a pattern which is relevant to the level of job on offer, the skills needed to meet the requirements of the job, and the type of candidate expected to be successful.

The most commonly used format involves taking you through your previous work or school life, with supplementary questions asked when and where necessary. This allows the interviewer to explore some areas in your application more thoroughly, or take up a point of interest arising from your previous answer. This type of interview is widely used for all levels and stages of selection interviewing and is probably what most candidates expect from an interview.

Other interviews, however, can involve a series of set questions aimed at finding out how you would react to particular situations which might arise in the job. These can be quite searching and are usually used for more senior posts. Such questioning needs careful answering because you must be able to substantiate your reply either by quoting a specific example of how you coped with a similar situation in the past, or by showing you would be able to tackle the problem through a logical, consistent approach. In these interviews, all candidates are asked the same questions.

Expect some note-taking when you answer. This is not a critical reaction but simply a way of ensuring the information you give is recorded properly for evaluation purposes later.

Timing
The professional recruiter will stand out a mile from the rest. The interview will start on time, take around half-an-hour to complete and leave you feeling you have had a fair hearing, done yourself proud and had all your own questions and queries resolved.

MAKING A GOOD ENTRANCE

Now you have some idea what to expect, it's time to consider your own part in the drama.

It's useful to think of the interview experience in terms of the dramatic. Like any good actor or actress, you have researched your subject, rehearsed your part, and dressed yourself up for the performance. Remember, to some extent during an interview you are acting out a role. This does not mean you are 'putting on an act', which is something entirely different and usually thought of as being false. As a candidate, you are putting all your best qualities to the fore and emphasising them. This is what is expected of you by your audience—your recruiters.

Curtain up will be from the moment your name is called.

Sometimes someone will come and collect you from the waiting area and escort you to the interview room. This is usually when the two locations are some distance apart and directions would be complicated or difficult to follow. If you are waiting in the area right next to the interview room however, you may simply be told that 'you can go in now'.

Introductions

As soon as you rise from your seat in the waiting area, *remember your personal presentation*. The spotlight for the next thirty minutes or so will be on you. Be aware of your surroundings immediately and act accordingly.

How should I handle the introductions?

- Treat the person who comes to escort you to the interview room as a potential interviewer—he or she often is.

- Remember his or her name when they introduce themselves.

- Take the lead from this person in making polite conversation. Keep replies brief and guard against making any negative comments about anything.

- Close the door behind you on entering the interview room if no one else does this for you.

- Make *eye contact* with everyone in the room.

- Smile!

- Listen to the name of the person being introduced.

- Remember it.

- Say 'hello'.

- Shake hands if this is expected.

- Sit down only when invited to.

- Put any bag or folders you are carrying on the floor to one side of your chair rather than on your lap. Murphy's Law will ensure they slide off at a crucial moment if you don't.

- Hold only your prepared question sheet and pen. This has the added advantage of keeping your hands occupied.

Initial questions

The purpose of these is simply to help you relax, and to start the essential process of building up a rapid rapport between you and your interviewer.

They have another basic purpose however, which is to give you the opportunity to hear your own voice in unfamiliar surroundings. *Pay attention to how you sound.* You may need to vary both the pitch and tone of your delivery to get the best results.

Heavily furnished rooms with thick carpets and curtains at the windows deaden your voice and you will need to speak a little louder and higher to compensate. This is not to say you should start shouting—simply make sure you can be heard. On the other hand, large rooms which are sparsely furnished tend to produce an echo. To counteract this you will need to speak slightly slower than usual, and also try to lower your pitch a little to reduce the tendency to 'squawk'.

Initial questions are always on very general subjects such as the weather or how you found your journey. When answering them, keep in mind their purpose. They are not part of the information gathering process so they should not be answered by long rambling speeches. Don't be tempted to review the climatic conditions of the past few weeks, or embark on a blow by blow account of the problems you encountered with your transport arrangements. If you do, two things will happen:

1. You will immediately bore your interviewer.
2. You will waste precious interview time.

- Keep your answers simple and to the point.

Gathering information

The interview begins in earnest when your interviewer starts expanding on the duties and responsibilities of the job, and where it fits into the **organisational structure**. This is sometimes prefaced by a brief description of the topics to be covered during the interview, but not always, so be prepared to plunge into the information section straight away.

- *Listen* and *concentrate* on what is being said.

- *Make notes*, particularly if the information which is being given answers some of your own queries, or seems to be important.

When you make notes, don't try to write down everything—you will find this impossible anyway unless you have the skills of a courtroom stenographer. Write down only those **key words** which help you remember the substance of what has been said. If you think you would find this difficult, practise by using news bulletins on the TV or radio; pick out the key words and put together the full story afterwards from what you have written. The type of words to look for are:

- natural headings such a 'training', 'duties', 'responsibilities'
- relevant 'action' words such as 'report to', 'complete by'
- qualifying words such as 'shortly', 'often'
- names and places
- numbers
- times and dates.

What will a good interviewer be looking for?
The primary objective of the interview is to identify the best person for the job, so expect some note-taking on the part of your interviewer to refresh his or her memory later on. Your suitability will be under the microscope and whether or not you are offered the post will depend on your having some or all of the following:

- qualifications
- experience
- motivation
- personality
- additional or **transferable skills**.

Your interviewer will also be looking for signs that you are:

- interested
- attentive

- communicative
- keen and (most important of all)
- able to show you have that 'something' extra.

How will my performance be judged by a good interviewer?
A good interviewer will be summing you up on several fronts at once;
by

1. what answers you gave to factual questions;
2. how you answered these questions;
3. how you responded to questions designed to encourage you to 'sell yourself' (the what-you've-done and how-you've-done it variety);
4. by your overall demeanour: appearance, awareness, decisiveness, politeness, humour, openness and so on.

Remember the importance of maintaining **eye contact** with the interviewer both while he or she is speaking and when it's your turn to answer questions. You do not have to stare fixedly, which is unnerving anyway, and in some circumstances positively intimidating. Good eye-contact can be maintained by moving your area of concentration within the triangle formed by the eyes and the end of the nose of a speaker. Before answering, it is perfectly acceptable to break eye-contact for a moment while you collect your thoughts, and re-establish it as you begin your reply.

ANSWERING BACKGROUND QUESTIONS

These set the stage. Some of them may seem obvious, others maybe less so. Some may be asked as a direct result of the analysis of your psychometric tests where the interviewer feels it would be useful to explore some aspects in greater depth. All questions have a purpose, however, so avoid showing any irritation just because you can't immediately see what lies behind them.

Questions about family
This is one of those areas which can not only cause embarrassment, but also irritation.

What, you may wonder, has the number of brothers or sisters you may or may not have, got to do with your application for a job? Does it matter that you are living with only one parent, or that both your parents are working full-time? Yes, it does.

If you have no previous employment history to put your achievements into some sort of perspective, questions on family background become important. You may have managed to obtain good grades in your examinations in spite of difficulties at home. You may have failed to reach the grades you wanted for the same reason. Your family circumstances therefore help your interviewer to see you as a complete person.

Questions about school and college

Basic facts about you
Basic factual information on your school achievements will be covered by details set out in your application, your record of achievement and from references or reports from your college or school. You may be asked at this stage to hand over any educational certificates for inspection with the promise that these will be returned to you later.

What your educational performance reveals
Your interviewer will not only want to question you on any obvious gaps between what you have to offer and what the job requires, he or she will also be looking at ways in which your performance at school or at college could reasonably be expected to reflect how you would perform in the world of work.

Problem areas
If there is any area of uncertainty contained in your references which indicates problems with punctuality, attendance or consistently poor performance in some subject, you can expect to be closely questioned on all of these topics.

Your perseverance
To check your level of perseverance when it comes to learning new and perhaps complicated tasks, you could well be asked which subjects you studied which you did not like or found difficult. If you managed to achieve a good result, so much the better.

Working individually or in a team
Your interviewer may feel it is important to suss out your ability to work as part of a team or on your own. To do this, he or she may want to know how you went about the task of completing project work and the contribution or lack of it from others.

Your self-image
How you see yourself is sometimes regarded as important. You may be asked whether you expected to do better or worse at a subject—and why.

Working with colleagues
If you are starting on the first rung of a trainee management ladder, you could well be asked for further details of your membership of school/college clubs, teams, societies etc and any positions held in them.

Hobbies and interests outside school or college

If there is little or no work experience on which to base assumptions about your **motivational drives** or attitude to work, what you choose to do in your free time assumes considerable importance.

Your interviewer will be looking for a well-balanced cross-section of activities, but not so great a commitment to one particular interest that your future career might suffer. This is the time when your nightly training sessions on the football field may have to give way to three nights a week at college studying for qualifications which will help you in your chosen career.

Interviewers will want to know what sparked off your leisure interests. What do you enjoy most about the time you spend on them? If you have recently given up a long-standing hobby, why did you decide to do so?

Questions on how much TV you watch—and what programmes in particular—are often seen as a minefield, and to some extent they are.

If you spend three or four hours a night in front of the TV regardless of what you are watching, your interviewer may classify you as 'a couch potato'—someone who lacks initiative, motivational drive, or who is simply downright lazy.

If you watch sports programmes but take no part in active sport, you give the impression you are prepared to stand on the side-lines and let others get on with the action. However, there is nothing wrong in saying you genuinely enjoy humorous programmes or even 'soaps'—as long as you can show you have a good reason for your preference. If you have spent the rest of your evening coping with school work and helping out looking after younger brothers or sisters, or an elderly relative, for example, you are entitled to some light entertainment.

Work experience

In this context, work experience is *not* the brief glimpse of working life you may have had as part of your school curriculum. Your interviewer will want to know more about long-term Saturday jobs, jobs taken during school or college holidays, or temporary jobs taken as 'fillers' until the right job opportunity came along.

Questions on work experience will be aimed at clarifying your attitude towards work and authority, your **motivational drives**, your enthusiasm towards training, a maturity through experience and an ability to cope and flourish within the work environment.

What sort of questions could I be asked about work experience?
Possible questions could be:

- What made you choose Acme Ltd for your holiday/Saturday job?
- What did you enjoy most about the job?
- [Where you have had several jobs] Which job did you enjoy most and why?
- Which job did you dislike most and why? [This is a very revealing question. If you think you could be asked this question, be sure you have worked out a very diplomatic answer in advance; avoid any comments which might be construed as criticism of named individuals.]

Additional questions

These usually refer to the nature of the job itself and any special needs associated with it, such as the need to be physically fit if there are strenuous duties involved, or your access to independent travel facilities if the job demands irregular or unsocial hours.

DANGER ZONES

What if I dry up?

This can happen even when someone is thoroughly well-prepared simply through stress, panic or being caught off guard.

Do – ask for the question to be repeated if necessary.
 – be honest if you genuinely cannot answer, but make sure you have a good reason for not being able to come up with something.

Don't – say the first thing that comes into your head—it's almost
    bound to be rubbish.
  – let the experience throw you off balance. Forget about it until
    later and concentrate on the next question.

Yes/No answers

Some questions will be **closed questions**, that is they will only require
'yes' or 'no' as an answer. However, there are occasions when you
may feel making such a bald statement does not fully explain a
situation or worse still, gives the wrong impression. Don't feel you
can't expand on your answer. For example:

Q. I see you got a Grade C for English.

A. Yes—I was disappointed/pleased because...

Keep your explanation limited to a simple, single sentence. If the
interviewer feels there is need for elaboration in the light of this, you
will be asked to expand on the topic further.

Giving negative answers

You may be placed in a position of having to give a negative reply
which seems to put you in a bad light. If you are, always try to
counterbalance this with a positive aspect. This may not always be
possible, but if you are concentrating on the line of questioning, you
may be able to see what the questioner is driving at. It could help you
put together a less downbeat response while giving an honest answer
at the same time. For example:

Q. Have you ever worked away from home before? (In other
    words—Will you be able to cope with organising your own life?)

A. No—but (giving reasons why you will be able to cope).

Finding fault with other people

This is an easy trap to fall into if you are wriggling to get out of an
awkward spot. You might for example be trying to explain away
poor academic performance or why you left an earlier job after only
two weeks.
    You may genuinely have had a teacher who lacked teaching
ability, or a boss who was impossible to get on with, but *never* say so.
If you do, you will give the impression you are ready to blame
someone else for your own shortcomings. You have also forewarned

your interviewer (who may be your potential boss) that you are likely to talk about him or her in the same way at sometime in the future. Worse still, if you name an individual, you are risking the possibility that this person might be well-known and well-respected by your interviewer.

Compulsive talking
This is sometimes caused by over-confidence, but is more likely the result of feeling stressed.

There are occasions when interviewers pause after you have answered a question, leaving you wondering if you should be saying something else—although you may have no idea what. It is very tempting to fill this silence, but if you feel you have answered the question as fully as possible, don't reduce the impact of your answer by unnecessary waffle.

Do – Recognise when you have said enough on a particular topic. Watch for clues from the interviewer—broken eye-contact, checking the time and so on.

– Avoid repeating yourself.

Don't – Interrupt the interviewer under any circumstances.

– Become irritated if the interviewer cuts you off in mid-sentence. Time is precious. Wasting time could cost you the job. The question you might have been asked if there had been time could have been the vital one.

Laughing
Don't! Smiling is fine, but giggling or misplaced laughter is not.

ASKING YOUR OWN QUESTIONS

When you are given the opportunity to put forward your own questions by the interviewer, this is a clear signal that the interview is drawing to a close.

If the interviewer is working to a tight schedule, you may not have time to ask more than two. With luck, some of your queries will already have been answered in the course of the interview, either during the initial background briefing, or as a result of additional information provided as back-up to questions you were asked.

How should I put my own questions?

1. Check through your list to identify queries which have still not been answered. Are there any new ones which have arisen as the result of the interview?

2. Choose the most important one to ask first with a second in reserve. Choose those which will help you decide whether you would accept the job if offered to you.

3. Ask only relevant questions. You may have listed several 'intelligent' queries some of which might have been answered during the interview. Resist the temptation to ask them anyway. You will give the impression you have not been paying attention.

If all your questions have been answered during the course of the interview, then *say so*, mentioning briefly which points had interested you. This shows you have given some thought to clarifying certain matters and that you are now satisfied the points have been adequately covered.

What things should I avoid?

1. Don't give the impression you never had any questions to ask in the first place.

2. Don't shrug your shoulders or pull a face. If you were the interviewer, how would you react to such a response?

HANDLING THE CLOSING STAGES

Once your questions have been answered, the interviewer will begin to close the proceedings. Usually he or she will tell you there are still other candidates to be seen, and give you some idea how long it will be before you are told the result. This can vary from the same day, to a few days or even longer.

If no timescale is mentioned, do ask when you can expect to be told. It will save you a great deal of anxiety later, and let you get on with the rest of your life without hanging around waiting for the phone to ring or the postman to call.

HOW TO MAKE A GOOD EXIT

The way you leave is just as important as the way you enter the interview, so make a good job of it.

Some basic tips

- Gather together the items you placed on the floor and ensure you have a tight grip on them.
- Stand up and straighten your clothes.
- Shake hands with your interviewer(s) if this is expected.
- Thank your interviewer(s) for their time.
- Smile.
- Make your exit by
  - stopping at the door
  - turning, smiling and thanking again
  - leaving, closing the door quietly behind you.

  The last impression of you should be a stunningly good one.

CHECKLIST

Analysing your performance after an interview:

1 Did you remember all the points as to personal presentation?
2. Did you make the right sort of entrance?
3. Did you establish good eye contact with the interviewer(s)?
4. Did you remember your interviewer(s)' name(s)?
5. Did you sit correctly?
6. How well did you concentrate on what was said?
7. Did you manage to keep looking keen, attentive and interested?
8. Did you really think clearly before answering?
9. Did you speak clearly?
10. Were you able to answer the questions that were asked?
11. Did you make yourself properly understood?
12. Were you able to clarify crucial areas of uncertainty about the job?
13. When will you be given the result of the interview?
14. Did you make a good impression on leaving?

7

The Problem Interview

WHAT CAN HAPPEN IN A DIFFICULT INTERVIEW?

Unfortunately, as was pointed out at the beginning of Chapter 6, many interviews fall short of the recognised high standards of the IPD.

It is important to avoid developing fixed ideas about what to expect from either your interview surroundings or your interviewer. Expectations can well suffer a nasty shock when reality strikes, and this will only add to your anxieties at a time when you want to keep them to a minimum. It is much better to approach your interview with an open mind. Expect *anything* and be mentally prepared to readjust your approach to adapt to any situation which might arise.

Timekeeping

Warning bells should start ringing if you arrive a quarter-of-an-hour before your appointment to find more than one other candidate in the waiting area. Something has gone badly wrong with the schedule, either because of an emergency, or more likely, because each interview is taking longer than the time originally allocated to it. This is sheer bad planning and can throw a carefully planned return journey home into total disarray.

Other areas of poor time-planning are:

- interviews restricted to too short a period—say quarter of an hour; or

- interviews extended beyond their 'natural' length—say beyond three-quarters of an hour.

A well-structured interview should last between half-an-hour and forty minutes, with five minutes allocated for the interviewer to complete any relevant notes before seeing the next candidate.

An unsuitable interview location

If you find yourself being ushered into a corner at the far end of a large office or workshop with hectic activity going on all around you unabated, you have problems. There could be several reasons for this unsuitable interview location, not all of them due to thoughtlessness:

1. There is no suitable spare room available to set aside for interviews.

2. Your interviewer is the supervisor in charge of a section, and can't, or won't, leave his or her work station for long periods.

3. Your interviewer is oblivious to the surroundings and does not think them unsatisfactory for interview purposes.

4. Your interviewer knows the surroundings are unsuitable but believes candidates should be able to cope with them.

Having your interview in a room shared with other members of staff can be just as harrowing. The effect is just the same as being interviewed in the larger environment—constant interruptions from both employees and phone calls to other people in the room.

Even where an interview room has been set aside from the hurly-burly of the rest of the organisation's everyday life, your troubles are not over. It may be any old spare room currently not being used. It may be the stationery cupboard or even a store room. Conditions may be cramped, vast, untidy, dirty, cold, hot, damp, stuffy, draughty or a combination of several of these. In other words, totally unsuitable.

Even in ideal surroundings, you can be faced with the 'interrogation' layout—a huge desk with three interviewers sitting behind it like judges, and the candidates' chair—rigid and straight-backed—placed several feet away from the table in terrible isolation.

All these signals warn of the low priority given to recruitment standards by the organisation, and may well reflect the management's attitude towards staffing matters in general.

Your interviewer(s)

One of the major problems with interviews is—as has been mentioned previously—that not all recruiters are professional personnel specialists, or well-versed in the interview standards expected by the **Institute of Personnel & Development**. Many are managers (supervisors, **line managers** or even departmental heads) who are experts in their own particular field—say in engineering or social work, for example—but who have only the barest understanding of what is required when recruiting staff. There are two possible reasons for this:

1. The organisation has no policy of ensuring that line managers involved in recruitment receive any training in even the most basic principles.

2. The individual manager concerned does not see the necessity for training, or has even resisted suggestions that it would be useful.

There are also occasions when even the best well-trained recruiters have their 'off' days. Perhaps he or she is going down with 'flu, or wrestling with personal worries; but whatever the problem it isn't going to help you get your case across to the maximum effect.

THE LESS-THAN-PERFECT INTERVIEWER

'I had it here somewhere'

There is nothing more dispiriting than finding yourself sitting opposite someone who is clearly disorganised or ill-prepared. Some of the danger signals to spot are:

- papers strewn untidily over the desk
- inability to find your application or associated papers
- vagueness about your name
- knows your name but nothing else about you
- scribbles notes on scrappy pieces of paper
- doesn't seem to know very much about the job on offer.

Why should the interviewer be in this state? Apart from the obvious reason of simply being poorly prepared or fundamentally unable to cope, here are a few others:

1. He or she may be a line manager who has only recently received all the relevant papers from the personnel department and has been unable to spend enough time preparing.

2. He or she may be a line manager whose mind is on day-to-day organisational problems rather than staff recruitment. As far as

this recruiter is concerned, recruitment should be somebody else's responsibility anyway.

3. The interviewer may be someone standing in at very short notice for a sick or absent colleague.

4. The interviewer may be a personnel officer conducting the interview without technical back-up from a line manager.

This last example is not necessarily something to worry about. If you find yourself in this situation, there is a good chance your technical abilities will be accepted. What is being sought is the right personality to fit the vacancy. In many non-technical posts, personnel officers interview candidates without any line manager back-up for the same reason. Once again it's you—not your qualifications for the job—which is under the microscope. But if you wanted answers to technical questions, you are going to be out of luck.

'Interviewing? There's nothing to it!'

This is the classic case of a line manager who believes he or she knows all there is to know on the subject of staff recruitment and who doesn't understand what all the fuss is about. Such individuals are usually supremely over-confident, but almost without exception are hopeless interviewers. Some are very conscious of their exalted status, or want to impress you with how busy they are. Be on the lookout for:

- The overwhelming hale and hearty approach.

- Aggressive or domineering questioning.

- A willingness both to be interrupted by telephone queries or individual members of staff, and to make you wait while the matter in hand is discussed, sometimes at great length.

- The expression of personal opinions in leading questions, for example 'I've no time for people who don't stand up for themselves, have you?'

- The habit of scoring points off you, for example 'When did you realise you were useless at Maths?'

- The openly discriminatory question or comment, such as 'Do you plan to carry on working after you get married?' (asked only of female candidates). Or 'We don't usually take on women/ blacks/Pakis here.' Or 'We weren't looking for a deaf data processor' when the job demands high levels of hand and eye co-ordination only.

This type of interviewer is unlikely to believe that they are anything less than brilliant in selecting the right candidate. He or she may even tell you how they usually make their choice. If you hear the words 'instinct' or 'hunch' used as a means of choosing the successful candidate, you know what you are up against. This is someone who only likes to have people working for him (or her) who will be yes-men (or women) or who reflect the boss's preferred outlook on life. You will therefore have a shrewd idea about the possible work environment you are letting yourself in for—and whether or not you would really want the job after all.

'I don't really enjoy interviewing and I don't know why I'm here.'

Here is an interviewer who feels very insecure and anxious about the whole procedure; someone like this should have been kept a million miles away from the recruitment process. What makes matters worse is that very often this interviewer's anxiety becomes infectious, reinforcing any nervousness you may already be experiencing.

The give-away signs

- nervous mannerisms such as throat clearing, pen fiddling, paper shuffling, lack of **eye contact** and rattling loose change or keys in pockets;

- excessive talking on unrelated topics because of uncertainty about what questions should be asked;

- sticking to a prepared stock of questions regardless of whether your previous answer has already covered the next point raised;

- failing to take up obvious supplementary questions which follow on naturally from the answer you have given;

- asking you to repeat factual information you have already given earlier;

- the consistent use of **closed questions** (where you can only answer 'yes' or 'no');

- the phrasing of questions pointing to the answer the interviewer wants to hear, for example 'Can I take it you enjoy working on your own?';

- a tendency to agree with everything you say; or

- the inability to take control of the interview at any stage.

Most interviewers in this category are specialist **line managers**; they know their limitations, have received no training to compensate and feel thoroughly out of their depth. But this is not the whole story. There are those for whom no amount of training would be of any use—particularly where the individual concerned has great difficulty relating to other people.

There is also the situation where an organisation recognises the need to give its line managers some basic recruitment instruction, but then adopts an unsatisfactory training programme which does little or nothing to improve interviewing standards. GIGO (garbage in, garbage out) applies to recruitment training as well as to computer data.

On the other hand, there are circumstances where the quality of training is excellent, but the individual manager is unwilling to abandon old habits for more updated methods.

HOW CAN I COPE WITH A PROBLEM INTERVIEW?

When you are faced with an interview where all the cards are stacked against you, all you can do is make the best of a bad job. A lot depends on how you cope, so the rules to follow are:

Recognise your predicament
What exactly is the problem? Timing, the place or the person? Are you going to be kept waiting longer than necessary? Is the interview venue unsuitable? Is the interviewer's approach unhelpful?

Try not to become flustered
Think positively. How can you overcome the difficulties you have identified? Can you overcome them? Make constructive use of any

time you have to kill, even if this means getting out of your seat and walking to the cloakroom two or three times. Treat interruptions during the interview or the unsuitability of the location as minor inconveniences. Handle your interviewer with care.

What about an aggressive or discriminating interviewer?

Coping with aggression
For your own peace of mind try to remain calm and retain your dignity if at all possible. Avoid getting into a direct confrontation if you can, especially if this is likely to degenerate into a heated argument. This may not be easy, as it is often difficult to hide personal anger or irritation under these circumstances, particularly if the behaviour of your interviewer is intolerable.

Coping with discrimination
If you feel by the manner of the questioning that you are being discriminated against on the grounds of your race or sex, or because of your disability, this is *unlawful*. In this situation, you really have only two choices:

1. Answer the question as best you can without rancour; or
2. Smile and suggest politely that the line of questioning is inappropriate.

Telling your interviewer that he or she is acting unlawfully, however, is not likely to improve matters. You will either inflame an already potentially explosive situation or produce acute embarrassment where the lapse was just the result of thoughtlessness. By antagonising or belittling your interviewer, you are in a no-win situation.

Walking out, by the way, is something you should only do as the last resort.

It's worth mentioning here, perhaps, that some interviewers think it's smart to harass a candidate to see how they respond under pressure, even though this is not recognised as good recruitment practice. Where the harassment is on a racial, sexual or disability basis, however, you have every right to take the matter further. You can seek help under the provisions of the **Race Relations Act 1976**, the **Sex Discrimination Act 1975** or the **Disability Discrimination Act 1995**. You will not be alone. You have only to look at the number of cases which continue to come before industrial tribunals and higher courts to realise there is still great ignorance of the legal obligations of employers in the field of recruitment and selection.

If you suspect or have good reason to believe you have been the subject of discrimination, the best time to act is when you receive confirmation that you have not been offered the job. If you feel the main reason for this is discrimination on the grounds of your race or ethnic origin, contact:

The Commission for Racial Equality
Elliot House
10–12 Allington Street
London SW1E 5EH   Tel: (0171) 828 7022

or on the grounds of your sex:

The Equal Opportunities Commission
Overseas House
Quay Street
Manchester M3 3HN   Tel: (0161) 833 9244

In the case of disability discrimination, no Commission for the Disabled was set up under the Disability Discrimination Act. Instead, complaints on the grounds of disability in England, Scotland and Wales are dealt with by the **Advisory, Conciliation and Arbitration Service (ACAS)**. ACAS was set up in 1975 to deal with a wide range of employment matters and operates on a regional basis. Your nearest public enquiry point will be listed in your local *Phone Book*. In Northern Ireland, the **Labour Relations Agency (LRA)** provides help on the same basis. Their address is:

The Labour Relations Agency
2/8 Gordon Street
Belfast
BT1 2LG   Tel: (01232) 321442

Holding you own when faced with a disorganised or anxious interviewer

In these circumstances, you can do a lot to help yourself provided you feel confident enough to take on the challenge. If you realise that your interviewer is in a bit of a state, your own approach can do a lot to help the situation.

- **Be patient**—it will be appreciated if your interviewer has been thrown into the deep end at a moment's notice.

- **Be helpful**—offer information which you think is both relevant and useful if your interviewer seems to have dried up or lost the drift of his or her questioning.

- **Be tactful**—avoid showing your contempt at what seems to be total incompetence or lack of professionalism.

- **Look encouraging**—this can work wonders if your interviewer is able to rescue the situation after an initially shaky start.

Anything you do to make your interviewer feel better will put you in a favourable light as far as he or she is concerned. It also says a great deal for your maturity, your level of awareness, your **interpersonal skills** and your ability to handle difficult situations. So don't blow your chances unnecessarily. Interviewers are human beings, too, and have their 'off' days like the rest of us.

CHECKLIST

1. What tell-tale signs are there that the interview process could be less than perfect?

2. Is your interviewer a line manager, or personnel officer? What can you tell from this?

3. Have you identified *all* the problem areas which could arise?

4. What are your plans to overcome or alleviate each problem identified?

5. Whatever happens, will you be able to set up and maintain a good rapport with your interviewer?

6. How would you handle a point of no return, where you felt you would have to speak out or leave?

8

The Waiting Game

HOW TO USE THE INTERVIEW EXPERIENCE

When you leave the interview room, your adrenalin level will still be quite high. You may find yourself experiencing all sorts of reactions from exhilaration and excitement to the deepest, darkest depression and a sense of anti-climax. Unless you make a positive effort, the valuable time immediately after your experience can be wasted.

If most of the interview seemed to go well, you may feel very confident and see no need to examine your performance. On the other hand, if it has been a disaster, the temptation to dwell too much on each catastrophe is almost overwhelming. In both cases, however, try to use the experience as a source of learning to perform better in future.

Why do I need to take stock?

There are very good reasons why you should stop and take stock of what happened as soon as possible after the event:

1. You may have more interviews in the near future and need to fix the events, personalities and facts associated with this one very firmly in your mind to prevent any possible confusion.

2. You need to be certain your personal presentation and performance were up to scratch. Were there any areas which unexpectedly let you down and need working on, or which were handled well and need remembering?

3. You need to be certain you have enough information to decide whether or not to accept the job if it were offered to you.

4. If things went badly, reviewing what happened helps you work through your tension, and if done thoroughly, should provide positive pointers on how to handle the next interview differently, and to better effect.

ASPECTS TO CONSIDER

These can be split into two categories:

- Have you enough information about the job?
- How do you rate your performance under real-life interview conditions?

WEIGHING UP THE JOB INFORMATION

Basic data about the job

This is the information you need before deciding whether or not to accept the job if it were offered to you. To begin with, ask yourself the following questions and write down your answers, or any questions that spring to mind.

1. Do I have details of ALL the crucial conditions of employment?
These include headings such as rates of pay, hours of work and so on as set out on page 41 in Chapter 3. If not, make a list of the outstanding matters that still need clarification.

2. Do I really understand what the job involves and what is expected of the successful candidate?
If for any reason some areas are still unclear, note these. Are they crucial factors which would affect whether or not you would take the job? If not, simply bear them in mind as questions which would need answering at some stage.

3. Were there any aspects of the job which the interviewer kept returning to?
If so, do you think you appreciate the significance of these? Do they point to areas of difficulty with a previous post-holder perhaps, or problems presented by the job itself, or do they reflect concern over aspects of your own candidature? Give some thought to these and make your notes clear for future reference.

4. Was there any information given to me during the interview which I omitted from my personal list of queries?
If so, should you include a question on this subject in future checklists, or was the information restricted to the job in question? Revise your checklist if necessary.

5. Do I know when and how I will be notified of the result?
Note this for future reference in your diary. Then, if there is some delay you can gauge when it would be appropriate for you to make enquiries.

Evaluating the data
Read through your notes several times before asking yourself the following questions. Write down your answers: it will help clarify your thinking.

1. Does the additional information gained during the interview change my original picture of the job?
Is this for better or worse—and why?

2. Was there anything about the interviewers or the workplace which affected how I felt about working for the organisation?
Was this for better or worse—and why?

3. If I received a telephoned offer of employment now would I be able to say 'yes' or 'no' immediately?
Which areas need clarification? Are there any other reservations (say level of pay for example) which you would prefer to have time to consider, or bring forward as points for negotiation?

Make sure your notes are clear and concise for easy reference. Keep them on top of the other papers relating to the job in their folder and have them ready to hand in case you need to discuss these items over the phone at short notice.

REVIEWING YOUR INTERVIEW

Reviewing the interviewer(s)
While the details are still fresh in your mind write down the name or names of your interviewer(s) together with their **job titles** if you did not know these previously—you may need to use these in subsequent letters or phone calls.

After each name and title write a short physical description to help you keep an image of the person concerned. Include any mannerisms in your description and what you believe his or her attitude was towards you. If you receive a call from your interviewer, fixing a quick mental picture of the person on the other end of the line should help the conversation run more smoothly.

Reviewing yourself

If you are to learn anything from looking back at your interview, it is crucial to be absolutely honest with yourself. Nothing will be achieved if you aren't. A personal performance questionnaire is set out for you to complete at the end of this section (page 96).

One of the most uncomfortable parts of any interview is when the interviewer or interviewers seem unhappy with the way you handle an answer to a particular question. If you experienced any of the following, they are usually warning signs that some aspect of your candidature is meeting with concern and casting doubts on your suitability to do the job:

- Was the interviewer repetitive, asking increasingly more pressing questions on the same topic?

- Was the subject being raised again by a second or even third interviewer later in the proceedings?

- Did the interviewer frown in response to your answer, or show other signs that all was not well, for instance, twisting or chewing the lips, raising an eyebrow without smiling or making 'I'm not sure about that' noises?

The reasons for these reactions could be:

1. You gave an inadequate reply
This could mean you did not provide enough detail or that your response was poorly thought out and woolly.

2. You misunderstood the question
In this case, your reply was confusing and an obstacle to the natural progression of the interview. The interviewer had first to back-track to rephrase the question, or help you through it in order to get the right sort of answer.

3. There is concern over your attitude
You have said or done something which has triggered negative vibrations—a flippant reply perhaps, or a thoughtless shrugging of the shoulders.

4. There is concern over your abilities

Somehow you have given the impression you would not be able to carry out the duties or responsibilities of the job—perhaps by drawing attention to possible problems or difficulties, instead of adopting a more positive approach.

What remedial action can I take?

There are several ways you can avoid this happening again:

- Clarify your answer to the problem question, or rethink this if you have not thought it through sufficiently.

- Learn to listen to the question being asked.

- Learn to answer the question being asked.

- If you were quizzed on a point of fact, could the problem be reduced by including more details in your application in future?

- Learn to control the urge to shrug or pull a face when unable to answer a question immediately.

- Learn to choose your words more carefully, avoiding the use of casual or off-hand comments, or words that carry too strong a meaning or echo a downbeat approach. What are your own reactions to answers such as—'It was OK', 'I suppose so', 'No way!', or 'I hated doing that'?

WAITING FOR THE RESULT

You may be desperately keen to get a particular job, but remember that unless there is more than one vacancy to fill, there is going to be only one successful candidate and several disappointed runners-up. During the waiting period, therefore, keep your job search going. You can always withdraw other applications later on if necessary. In the meantime, keep a positive attitude and avoid making the mistake of telling yourself getting this job is a do-or-die situation. You will only leave yourself wide open to crushing disappointment if someone else is appointed.

PERSONAL PERFORMANCE REVIEW

1. Did I arrive on time   Yes/No
2. Did I allow enough time to freshen up?   Yes/No
3. Did I choose the right interview outfit?   Yes/No
4. Was there anything I would change next time?   Yes/No
5. If Yes, what? ....
   ....
6. Did I have problems with the test?   Yes/No
7. If Yes, list what these were ....
   ....
   ....
8. How would I overcome these problems next time?
   ....
   ....
9. A list of *all* my actions from the time I entered
   the interview room up until the interview began.
   ....
   ....
   ....
   ....
10. Was there anything I forgot to do? (See Chapter 5)   Yes/No
11. If Yes, what ....
    ....
12. Could I have improved anything?   Yes/No
13. If Yes, what? ....
    ....
14. Do I feel I settled quickly?   Yes/No
15. If No, why not?..
    ....
16. Did I feel there was a good rapport between
    me and the interviewer?   Yes/No
17. If No, why not?..
    ....
18. Is there anything I could do to prevent this
    happening again? ....
19. What was the most difficult question?......................
    ....
20. How did I handle it?   Well/So-so/Badly

21. If Well, what answer did I give? ....

    ....

    ....

22. If So-so, how would I change my reply if I were
    asked the same question again? ....

    ....

    ....

23. If Badly, what answer would I give if I were asked
    the same question again? ....

    ....

    ....

24. At any stage did I drop a 'clanger'?   Yes/No
25. If Yes, what was it? ....

    ....

26. How could I avoid doing this in future? ....

    ....

    ....

27. Were the questions *I* asked appropriate?   Yes/No
28. If No, why did I ask them? ....

    ....

29. A list of *all* my actions from the moment the interview
    closed until the time I was outside the interview room.

    ....

    ....

    ....

30. Was there anything I forgot to do? (See Chapter 5).   Yes/No
31. If Yes, what? ....

    ....

32. Do I still feel the interview as a whole went well
    or badly and why? ....

    ....

    ....

    ....

Note When you have completed the questionnaire, you should have a more precise picture of the good and the bad points of your performance which can be used to help you in the future.

Should I make the first approach?

This is a very debatable point. The greatest danger lies in being tempted to write an enthusiastic letter the day after the interview. The idea behind this seems to be to impress your recruiters, emphasising how much you would like to be considered for the job and your willingness to be available immediately.

Be warned that with some recruiters this sort of approach will go down like a brick. So avoid it. It is far better to leave your interviewers to make up their own minds than damage your chances by being labelled a creep.

The time to begin thinking about contacting your potential employers is once the deadline for hearing the result has passed. You are then perfectly within your rights to make a tentative enquiry to find out whether the decision will be made shortly.

Does silence mean anything?

You may have been told to expect a delay of a week or so before hearing the result: but if you have not heard within two or three days after your interview, this usually means that someone else has been offered the post.

All is not lost, however. There is always some delay between the successful candidate being offered the job and he or she accepting it. Until an employer has received this acceptance in writing, the remaining candidates have to be kept waiting. The reason is that the successful candidate does not always take up the offer, in which case the next best candidate will be approached.

How should I make the approach?

Once you have decided you want to know one way or the other, contacting the organisation by phone is obviously the quickest way of being put out of your misery. It does have its drawbacks, however.

1. Can I cope with receiving bad news over the phone?
There is something chillingly clinical about a ten second conversation which is the mental equivalent of having a bucket of ice-cold water thrown over you.

2. Am I ready to be put on the spot?
You may have phoned just at the right time—the letter is being drafted at that very moment offering you the job. Consequently, you may be expected to give an immediate response, or be faced with the complexities of negotiating some aspect of the offer which you might not be ready for.

3. Would I accept the job on the spot if it were offered to me?
If the answer is an unqualified yes, then go ahead and make the call.

If you don't feel up to coping with hearing the good or bad news in a matter of a few tension-filled seconds, then writing a letter is the only alternative. Keep it brief and to the point along the lines suggested on page 100.

The obvious disadvantage of writing a letter, of course, is that you are kept on tenterhooks for several more days waiting for a reply.

BECOMING THE SUCCESSFUL CANDIDATE

Congratulations! Now—how do you handle success?

The telephoned offer

Here you are being put on the spot. Your immediate reaction is probably one of such excitement, it is difficult to put your thoughts into any sensible order. *Stay calm* and consider the following questions:

- Can you give an unqualified 'yes' to the offer?
- Are there any points you noted down previously which need to be raised?
- Are you happy with the replies you are given?

The unqualified 'yes'
This is the ideal situation: you know all the conditions of service, the duties and responsibilities of the job, and feel confident you are the right person to take it on.

Unanswered questions
These are queries you noted down when you completed your review which are crucial to helping you decide whether or not you want the job.

If you have been businesslike in your approach to the job search, the relevant papers with the queries on top of them will be to hand in the folder in your filing system. Go through these with your contact and *write down* the answers. Don't trust yourself to remember all the details later on, even immediately after the phone call has finished. In a heightened state of excitement it's easy to miss a vital piece of information.

Your Ref:
ET(T)/ED/357/PE/Ed

46 Longworth Road
Martonley
Chillingham
CH17 5RH

26 January 199X

For the attention of Mrs Edwards

Dear Mr Raine

Appointment of Engineering Technician (Trainee)

I am writing in connection with the interviews for the above vacancy which took place on 13 January.

At the time, I understood from Mr Sharples, Divisional Engineer, that I would hear the result within two weeks.

As I have not yet heard from you, I was wondering if you could now let me know if I have been successful on this occasion.

Yours sincerely
Maxine Roberts (Miss)

Mr W. P. Raine
Chief Personnel Officer
Fenham & Massey Ltd
Fenham House
27 Victoria Road
Chillingham
CH3 9XQ

Are you happy with everything?
This applies not only to the answers you receive in response to your queries, but also to the offer which is made to you.

You may now discover that the rate of pay on offer is less than you expected. This usually occurs when a job is allocated a grade with several pay levels within it. Precisely where you will be placed depends largely on your age, qualifications and/or experience. It might also be subject to upward revision after you finish a probationary period or gain a recognised qualification.

Unfortunately, some employers have a policy of placing the newcomer on the lowest possible payment level. Unless you have an extremely good case for arguing otherwise, there is little room for manoeuvre. Like it or lump it.

The unqualified 'no'
It may seem strange to reach this stage and be in the position of saying 'no' to a job offer—but it can happen. Here are some reasons why:

- You have just been offered a better job elsewhere.
- Your personal circumstances have suddenly and unexpectedly changed.
- Now you know more about the job, it has less appeal than when you applied for it.
- The **conditions of employment** have been varied from those originally set out, and are less advantageous.
- Having met him or her, you are certain you will be unable to get on with your superior (although it would be diplomatic to give an alternative reason).
- There will be little or no opportunity to receive training or promotion as you were led to believe.
- You are being offered less than the going rate for the job elsewhere.

(If you decide not to pursue your application before the time you expect to hear the result of your interview, always tell the organisation concerned as soon as possible. This is only courteous and saves unnecessary consideration of your application. If you have not been given the result of your interview within the specified time however, you are under less of an obligation to advise them of your decision.)

If you have to say no, say it politely and thank everyone for their time and trouble. You might want to apply for another position with the same organisation at some time in the future.

The possibly 'yes'
If you are in doubt about giving a reply straight away, don't be pushed into accepting unconditionally on the spot. By all means say you would like to accept the offer, but subject to receiving written details.

This gives you more time to think through aspects you might be uncertain about and come to a more balanced decision.

The written offer

An example of a letter offering employment is set out opposite. The great advantage of receiving a written offer is that you are allowed the luxury of spending more time to think out your reply. However, if you are asked to confirm or decline the offer by a certain date, then only circumstances beyond your control should prevent you from meeting this deadline. Remember, other candidates are being held in suspense in the meantime.

Read through the information you have been given in the letter and any documents which might have been sent with it. Next, go through the headings considered under 'The telephoned offer' earlier in the chapter, and be certain you can take up the appointment based on the information you have to hand. Are there still unresolved queries which need clarifying? If so, take these up on the telephone rather than enter into a long-winded correspondence, particularly if you want to negotiate the rate of pay, or the date suggested for you to start work.

How do I agree to an offer in writing?

Any important letter should be roughed out in draft form. Don't send the final version until you are satisfied it says everything you want it to say in the proper manner.

Make a note of the points you have to cover in agreeing to take up the post, such as

- pay and conditions
- starting date
- any additional points such as meeting a named person at a stated time, or acknowledging attendance at an introductory meeting with new colleagues.

Keep your letter concise and to the point, paying attention to

- using the correct form of address eg Dear Mr, Ms, Mrs, Miss... Yours sincerely
- addressing it to the right person
- quoting any references used.

FENHAM & MASSEY LTD

Head Office
Fenham House, 27 Victoria Road
Chillingham, CH3 9XQ

Telephone: (01234) 70707
Fax: (01234) 70717

My Ref: ET(T)/ED/357/PE/td   **This matter is being dealt with by:**
Your Ref: Mrs P Edwards   **Ext:** 2439

31 January 199X

Dear Maxine

Appointment of Engineering Technician (Trainee)

Thank you for your letter of 26 January. I now have much pleasure in being able to offer you the above post at our Martonby engineering site.

Your rate of pay will commence at £95.00 per week rising to £100.00 per week on completion of a satisfactory six month probationary period. Full details of other conditions of service are set out on the attached sheet. If you are prepared to accept the appointment on the terms and conditions as set out, I should be grateful if you would let me know in writing no later than 10 February 199X.

At the same time, could you also confirm that you would be able to start on Monday, 14 February 199X. If this is convenient, I shall make arrangements for Mr Quinn, the Health and Safety Officer, to meet you at the South Gate Reception Area at 8.30 a.m. to arrange for you to be provided with suitable safety equipment before handing you over to Mr Konieczny, your section head.

May I take this opportunity of welcoming you to Fenham & Massey and hope you will enjoy working for the firm.

Yours sincerely

W P Raine

W P Raine
Chief Personnel Officer

Miss M Roberts
46 Longworth Road
Martonby
Chillingham CH17 5RH

Keep a copy of your letter and pin it to the front of your papers in your job file. Your **career history** starts here, so keep these papers in a safe place for future reference purposes.

For practice, re-read the letter Maxine has received from Fenham & Massey Ltd and draft out how you would respond if you were accepting the offer. A sample letter is set out below.

Your Ref:
ET(T)/ED/357/PE/td

46 Longworth Road
Martonby
Chillingham
CH17 5RH

3 February 199X

For the attention of Mrs Edwards

Dear Mr Raine

Appointment of Engineering Technician (trainee)

Thank you for your letter of 31 January offering me the above post.

I am happy to accept this on the terms and conditions set out in your letter, and can confirm I shall be able to start on Monday, 14 February 199X at 8.30 am, when Mr Quinn, the Health and Safety Officer, will meet me at the South Gate Reception Area.

I am very much looking forward to starting my career with Fenham & Massey.

Yours sincerely
Maxine Roberts (Miss)

Mr W.P. Raine
Chief Personnel Officer
Fenham & Massey
Fenham House
27 Victoria Road
Chillingham
CH3 9XQ

How should I decline an offer in writing?
If you have to decline the offer, do so politely. Never jeopardise your future employment chances.

As with a telephoned offer, you will be expected to give sound reasons for your decision because recruiting staff is an expensive business and time-wasters are not at all popular.

Just as you would draft out an acceptance letter to ensure you produced a finished product you can be proud of, treat your letter turning down the offer to the same meticulous attention. Keep a copy on file for record purposes; retain the folder until you are absolutely certain you won't need to refer to it again.

An example of how Maxine might have declined Fenham & Massey's offer is set out overleaf.

CHECKLIST

1. Do you have all the data you need to accept the job? If not, what else do you need to know?

2. Have you made a handy reference note of any queries?

3. Have you noted the name(s) and title(s) of your interviewer(s) for future reference?

4. Have you completed the questionnaire on your performance?

5. Have you made a list of any points you need to work on?

6. How do you intend to improve these?

7. Were there any aspects of your application which seemed to worry the interviewer?

8. Can you overcome these in the future?

9. What aspects of your personal presentation would you wish to change in future?

10. Do you feel it is the right time to enquire about the result of the interview?

11. If you tackle this by phone, have you got all your essential documentation to hand for negotiation or discussion purposes?

12. Have you been offered the job with conditions you can accept?

13. Have you to accept/refuse the job by a certain date?

46 Longworth Road
Martonby
Chillingham
CH17 5RH

3 February 199X

For the attention of Mrs Edwards

Dear Mr Raine

Appointment of Engineering Technician (Trainee)

Thank you for your letter of 31 January offering me the above post.

I very much regret I am unable to take up your offer as I have just accepted a similar post with Topham Engineering in Roxstead, starting next week.

Thank you again for giving me the opportunity to join Fenham & Massey. I am sorry I am unable to do so on this occasion.

Yours sincerely
Maxine Roberts (Miss)

Mr W.P. Raine
Chief Personnel Officer
Fenham & Massey
Fenham House
27 Victoria Road
Chillingham
CH3 9XQ

9

Factors Beyond Your Control

One of the most difficult situations you have to face during the job search is when you are confident you handled everything perfectly, there was a wonderful rapport between you and your interviewer and—*bang*, four days later you are shot down in flames by a three-line standard rejection letter.

WHAT WENT WRONG?

Although it won't lessen the feeling of being utterly crushed, it sometimes helps to know some of the possible reasons why you weren't chosen.

Your lack of success this time could be due to any one or more of the following:

- the next candidate
- interpersonal chemistry
- the non-existent vacancy
- your interviewer's hidden incompetence
- the right person–wrong workplace situation.

What can we learn from each of these?

The next candidate
You may indeed have given a good account of yourself during the interview; your sense of well-being may have been reinforced by your interviewer's enthusiastic response, giving you the impression you were home and dry. This positive reaction to your performance was probably perfectly genuine. Up until then you were very likely the best candidate. Unfortunately, this happy state of affairs did not last long. You were only the best candidate until the one who came after you seemed even better.

You may have been pipped at the post by only a whisker, but it is a sad fact of recruitment that runners-up are rarely told how close they came to being successful.

Interpersonal chemistry

Here is a situation where two candidates of equal merit leave the recruiter in a quandary. Which one should be chosen? The answer is simple—the candidate with whom the interviewer instinctively felt more comfortable.

There is nothing you can do to affect this type of decision. We all consciously or subconsciously like one person more than another. It is only natural that recruiters, too, will choose the person they instinctively warmed to in preference to someone who perhaps did not have quite the same 'aura'.

The non-existent vacancy

This is a real time-waster. Despite the costs involved in recruitment, there are still some jobs advertised which are already unofficially ear-marked for an **in-house candidate**—someone already employed by the organisation concerned. This may sound a crazy situation; it reflects the lack of proper career and promotion policies within these organisations—notably in the public sector—where an existing member of staff is obliged to compete with outside applicants for a vacant post.

If you are **short listed** under these circumstances, you will simply be in the business of making up numbers.

What makes matters worse is that such interviews can go with a swing. This is because the interviewers are not operating under the stress of having to genuinely pick out the best candidate. They feel relaxed, the atmosphere is good-natured and friendly, and you come away lulled into a false sense of security.

If you want to check out whether any in-house candidates have been short-listed, there is no harm in asking before you attend. At least this way you are half-prepared if things go wrong later.

Don't assume, however, that if there is an in-house candidate, your chances are doomed from the start. There are occasions when the result is not a foregone conclusion. The existing employee may be looking for a change of scene without having the necessary experience or skills when it comes to the crunch. Or, the line manager may be obliged to interview the in-house candidate because of trade union agreements with the employer. Finding out if there are such agreements could be a useful exercise if you are applying for a post with an employer where trade union members form a large percentage of the workforce.

Your Interviewer's hidden incompetence

Here is a situation where, if you had seen how your application was handled once you left the interview room, you might have had some inkling as to what went wrong with what seemed a first-rate interview.

Some recruiters are excellent at asking all the right questions to get the best from a candidate, but lack the essential back-up of good organisational skills and ability to make a proper assessment afterwards.

Inadequate recording of answers, imprecise judgements of performance and allowing too little time between candidates for a proper assessment to be made, can all add up to disaster as far as you are concerned.

You will never know when something like this ruins your chances, and there is really nothing you can do to prevent it happening.

Right person – wrong workplace

In these circumstances your interviewer believed you were everything the organisation had been looking for BUT.... To put it bluntly, this big 'but' is where you simply would not fit into the existing workforce.

You may be applying for a job which for historical reasons has always attracted a particular type of applicant. For instance, caring posts in the past have been predominantly held by women, whereas building work has been dominated by men. If you don't match the stereotyped image, you are likely to face an uphill struggle to become the successful candidate.

The male typist, the female mechanic, and where you are definitely the odd one out because of your race or colour, are all examples of potential problem areas. Without knowing the level of competence of the successful candidate, it is hard to prove that your sex or colour (or both) prevented you from getting the job.

Discrimination may not stem from any prejudice on the part of your interviewer. The danger zone might lie elsewhere, for example with the **group culture** that already exists in the section where the vacancy has arisen. Your interviewer may have foreseen problems in trying to fit you into a situation where dominant personalities could prevent your acceptance by the group. In this case, unless you had a chance to see and meet your potential colleagues, and of gauging their reaction to you, you will only be guessing that some form of discrimination lay behind your rejection.

In an ideal world, of course, the personnel officer or line manager would simply say you were the best candidate and go ahead and offer you the job. But life is never that simple. It is not always easy to change an existing work culture, even with the best of intentions. Throwing the hapless individual in at the deep end as the guinea pig is not an ideal way of going about it.

If you do feel very strongly that your application has not succeeded because of discrimination on the grounds of sex, race or disability, and you have proof (documents or witnesses) to back this up, seek the advice of the **Equal Opportunities Commission** the **Commission for Racial Equality**, or the **Advisory, Conciliation and Arbitration Service**, (or in Northern Ireland, the **Labour Relations Agency**). How to contact these organisations is set out on page 89 in Chapter 7 and in the list of Useful Addresses at the end of the book.

HOW TO SALVAGE YOUR PRIDE

Here are some tips for salvaging your pride:

Don't be disheartened
This is easier to say than to achieve, but if you can genuinely tell yourself that you did your best, be philosophical and look on the occasion as an opportunity to try for something better.

Don't let your standards drop
Disappointment, disillusionment and disgust can undermine a positive approach. Whatever went wrong this time, it must not affect the way you continue your job search. Every new interview must be treated with the same attention to detail as the first. Only this way will you eventually find success.

Continue your job search with a thorough and carefully researched approach
The more interviews you attend, the greater should be your overall knowledge of competitors operating in the same sector of industry, commerce or public service. This will help you make better judgements of various employers and what they have to offer.

Consider every interview as an opportunity to show yourself off to your best advantage
You might not succeed in obtaining the job you applied for, but a

recruiter can sometimes be sufficiently impressed to offer you an alternative opening.

Think of every interview as a learning experience on which to build for the future
Learning to handle yourself in stressful situations can be of benefit in other interview circumstances, such as going to the doctors, meeting your bank manager or having to attend a court of law.

COPING WITH CONTINUOUS REJECTION

If you have been struggling with your job search for six months or more and attended a whole series of interviews without success, it may be time to take stock of the situation. One of your options is to consult your local careers service providers who exist to help young people in full-time and part-time education and those under 18 who are unemployed. In some cases they also give help to adults and those who have taken career breaks and want to return to work. They can advise you on your career choice and help you develop job search skills.

In the last few years the careers service has been taken out of local authority control to operate either in partnership with a TEC or more recently by private companies. As a result, what services are on offer in your area will not necessarily appear under *Careers Service* in the telephone directory and you should contact either your local TEC (or LEC) or nearest Jobcentre for this information.

It may be that without knowing it, you have been trying to find work in the wrong sort of employment. This is easily done when you start your job search because you tend to concentrate on finding jobs to match only your skills and qualifications. Important though these are, they are only part of the story.

Matching more than just skills and qualifications
Consider the following range of occupations. What can they possibly have in common?

Architectural technician	Pharmacy technician
Bank/building society clerk	Statistician
Dental hygienist	Textile technician
Engineering maintenance worker	Veterinary nurse
Merchant navy deck officer	

The answer? A good GCSE pass in science or maths.

You can see from this list (which is far from complete by the way) that jobs requiring basic qualifications can offer a tremendous variety of work environments and career prospects. They cater for the person who likes working alone, or enjoys working as part of a team; for the person with creative flair, or steady persistence; for the office worker, or the person who wants to travel the world; for the sociable sort who likes meeting people, or someone who prefers to work with animals; for the person skilled with their hands, or someone academically inclined.

The right choice of job depends not *just* on qualifications but on personal motivation and preferences, too. You may not even know that some of these exist and this is where the careers service providers can help. He or she will be able to advise you on alternative opportunities to match your *personality* as well as your skills and abilities.

You may discover that your preferred job calls for additional qualifications, or better grades, and you may need to consider a spell of further education to help you attain your objective. Alternatively, after giving the matter thought, you may feel you would be better setting up in business on your own. (Going to college and starting up in business are topics covered in the next two chapters.)

Getting other well qualified help and advice
If after your discussion with the careers adviser, you still do not know what to do for the best, then it may be time to seek the advice of an **occupational psychologist**. Career Analysts in London, for example, has a staff of well qualified occupational psychologists, working mainly with 15-24 year olds. The firm has been established since 1965 and has a high reputation for providing sound advice and counselling at a reasonable cost. Each year, around 3,000 young people use their services to sort out educational and career problems when all else has failed.

Counselling is confidential. It is based on results from a range of **psychometric tests** which are broadly similar to those used by many larger firms for recruiting staff. A comprehensive report is prepared giving practical guidance and there is a follow-up questionnaire to check your progress two years afterwards. If you want further information on the careers guidance available, write to:

Career Analysts
Career House
90 Gloucester Place
London W1H 4BL
Tel: (0171) 935 5452. Fax: (0171) 486 9922.

All is not lost. Sometimes the problem just has to be tackled in a different way. All you need is the right sort of guidance to help you do just that.

CHECKLIST

1. Were you 100% satisfied with your performance during the interview?

2. Was there anything you saw, heard, or which happened before, during or after your interview which might explain your rejection?

3. Was there an in-house candidate?

4. Were you applying for a job which might have a gender stereotype?

5. Are there any grounds for pursuing action against your interviewer under the Race Relations, Sex Discrimination or Disability Discrimination Acts?

6. Are you trying for the wrong sort of job?

7. Could you make a list of what alternatives are available?

8. Would you be better improving your qualifications?

9. How would you go about this?

10. Should you perhaps be thinking about working for yourself?

10

College Interviews

WHEN THE INTERVIEW PLAYS A DECISIVE ROLE

Not all offers of a college place depend solely on obtaining the right grades in your examination results. In some cases, these are simply the first rung of the ladder. You may be expected to sit further tests, or to 'pass' an interview before being offered a place.

Where colleges offer courses in specific areas of activity, such as drama, teacher training, agriculture or marine electronics, the interview is an integral part of the selection procedure. The more prestigious the college, the more rigorous the entry requirements. The same can be said when a course has more candidates than places available, and the college is able to pick and choose from the best of those applying.

If you are in a competitive situation with a college interview, rather than simply going through a ritual acceptance procedure, you need to be prepared to adopt the right approach to be successful.

'YOU ARE INVITED TO ATTEND...'

What does this mean to the college?

Basically, the college has sifted through the applications and decided they like the 'look' of you. They want to choose the best from a pool of possibles and on the face of it, you have the makings of being a successful student.

Colleges want successful students, particularly where they are seeking to maintain a high standard or a national reputation for producing first-rate, employable 'graduates'. Specialist colleges in particular are concerned to minimise the drop-out rate on courses. They will therefore do everything possible to ensure that, barring unforeseen circumstances, the students allocated places will literally 'stay the course'.

What does this mean to me?

Being invited to a college interview means exactly the same as being invited to a job interview—you have crossed the first selection hurdle. From now on, you need to be ready to demonstrate that 'something' extra that will lift *your* candidature above the rest. More importantly, you need to be very clear in your mind why you have chosen that particular college to further your intended career, and why you have chosen that particular career in the first place. If you fudge either issue, you could be in for trouble.

THE LETTER OF INVITATION

This is no different in principle from the letter inviting you to a job interview. It should tell you everything you need to know to plan ahead:

* date, time and place of interview
* whether you will be required to take some form of test
* what documents you should take with you
* who will meet you
* travelling and/or lodging expenses
* who and how to contact to confirm attendance.

Date, time and place of interview

College interviews almost always involve either half-a-day or a whole day visit to the college premises. This gives candidates a chance to look round, meet the staff and sometimes students already established on their courses. It also allows college staff to see how you respond to the surroundings and the people you meet.

Attending a college interview is much more likely than a job interview to involve long-distance travel arrangements, or even an overnight stay. You will need to start making enquiries as soon as possible to cover both these points so that any problems can be sorted out with the college at the time you write or telephone to confirm your attendance.

Will I be expected to take a test?

For some technical courses, you may be expected to take an entrance examination. This will be designed to overcome the problems of varying subject content in the curricula options offered by the various GCSE Examining Boards, which make comparison between students difficult.

A college specialising in the performing arts will naturally expect you to demonstrate your ability at an audition.

Your letter should tell you whether you need to take any equipment with you. Be sure to act on this.

What documents should I take?

Even if these are not specified, always take with you:

- any educational certificates
- your record of achievement
- any relevant project work completed either at school or at home as part of a hobby.

References from a previous employer or your head teacher are usually taken up direct by the college. However, if you have a testimonial from some other person of authority to support your application, then there is no harm in taking this along with you and offering it for inspection at the appropriate time.

Will someone meet me?

Your instructions might simply tell you to report at the enquiry office or reception area at a particular time. However, some colleges like to greet potential students on a more personal basis. You may therefore be met by a member of staff, or a student in his or her final year, or both. One or other will then show you round the college, make any necessary introductions and take you to the waiting area. If there is to be an examination or test the candidates will probably all take it at the same time for ease of administration. You could have a lot of hanging around to do before you go in for your interview proper.

What about travelling/lodging expenses?

You will need to check whether you are expected to meet these expenses out of your own pocket or whether expenses are paid only for certain types of transport. If this is not mentioned in the letter, contact the college administration department and clarify the situation well in advance.

How should I reply to the letter?

Treat your response to a college interview just as you would for a job interview (see Chapter 1).

- Check your personal availability at the time and date suggested.

- Negotiate a new time and date if either or both present *insurmountable* problems.

- Clarify any points in the letter which you may not fully understand, or take up any queries you may have.

- Confirm your attendance in the manner requested.

PERSONAL PRESENTATION

What should I wear?

The 'scruffy' student image is not as acceptable as might be imagined. In college interviews a good personal presentation is still expected both in what you wear and how you look.

If you are applying for a place in a college associated with the performing arts, then a certain amount of flamboyance is expected— it is part and parcel of your 'image' building. But for most interviews it simply doesn't pay to turn up looking like a multi-coloured tramp. Dress in casual wear by all means, but let it be clean—never scruffy or threadbare. The way you dress and maintain yourself says something about your state of mind. If you can't be bothered to present yourself properly, you will give the impression this is how you will approach your work. As mentioned earlier in the chapter, colleges want successful students, not potential drop-outs.

In some colleges, particularly those with strong authoritarian traditions or where you will be issued with a uniform, you will be expected to turn up smartly dressed and well groomed. Anything less will be unacceptable.

Some general tips on appearance

1. Regard personal cleanliness as important.

2. Wear clothes which give the impression they are clean and in reasonably good condition.

3. Don't set out to use the interview as a platform for making an obscure personal statement on life or anything else. This is not the time or place.

4. Don't expect universal enthusiasm for personal idiosyncrasies.

Acting the part

Go back to Chapter 2 and refresh your memory on how this should be approached to show yourself off to the best advantage. Pay special attention to:

- nervous mannerisms and irritating habits
- bad posture when walking, standing or sitting
- negative body language that contradicts what you are saying
- mumbling, indistinct speech, or poor content, with over-fondness for meaningless phrases or 'you-knows'.

As with job interview preparation, take any remedial action which might be necessary and work at it.

BACKGROUND PREPARATION

Basic groundwork is just as important for competitive college interviews as it is when you are going for a job. This research not only helps you to be sure you are applying for the right reasons but also confirms your commitment in the eyes of the college. A college, particularly one which specialises, will be looking for students who can demonstrate all of the following:

- A clear understanding of what they want to do with their lives.

- Evidence of thorough research into the educational needs of their chosen careers.

- Evidence of detailed comparisons of all the courses available to pursue those careers.

- The choice of college for the quality or type of course on offer.

- The motivation to complete the course once started, come what may.

- The self-awareness to know they have the right personality for the career they have chosen.

- Proof that the interest is genuine by efforts to obtain work experience in related fields.

- The potential to complete the course successfully.

- The intention to follow a career relevant to the course applied for.

With these requirements in mind, therefore, write down your own reasons for the following:

1. Why did you choose this particular course?

2. Why did you choose this particular college in preference to any other?

Leading on from this, write down how you would be able to show from your school work, hobbies, leisure interests or work experience:

3. Your competence to complete the course successfully.

4. Your motivation to do so.

5. Your commitment to following up the course with an appropriate career.

Questions to ask yourself

Looking at the reasons you have given for choosing the course, are these reasons clear, valid and justifiable, or do they give the impression of woolly-mindedness?

Does some difficulty lie in the fact you are unclear about certain aspects of the course? If this is the case, write these down separately so you can clarify them during the interview.

What about your choice of college? Did you find out which colleges offered the relevant course you were interested in, and compare their prospectuses to find the one best suited to you? Your reasons for choosing this particular college should be valid from both an educational and college point of view. Reasons such as 'my best friend has applied', or 'it's a nice part of the country', might be true, but they are unlikely to cut much ice with your interviewer.

Importance of showing the right attitude

How can you demonstrate your potential to complete a course

successfully? The answer lies in your attitude to school work and your approach to study. With this in mind ask yourself the following and write down the answers:

- Does my record of achievement and/or educational certificates reflect a positive picture?

- Are there any areas of poor or less than satisfactory performance?

- Do I have valid reasons to explain these, such as sickness, family mobility or domestic crises?

- Are there any areas where I know my performance is weak? Would it be better to honestly admit this and recognise the need to work harder to improve?

- Is there any way I can demonstrate that I would be able to rectify these problems in future?

Next, think about what motivated you to decide to take the course. The specialist colleges in particular want students who have really thought through their career goals and are not just filling in time hoping something will turn up at the end of it all. Some take pride in the percentage of students who successfully complete their courses and go straight into related employment.

Your interviewers will be looking for *evidence* that you really sought appropriate work experience opportunities in your chosen field, whether in the form of a temporary job, evening work, a Saturday job or a holiday placement.

Questions to ask yourself on work experience
Look at the questions below and ask yourself if the answers really do support your application:

- Does your work experience reflect your enthusiasm to pursue a career relevant to the course?

- If not, what reasons can you give to explain this and are they valid? For example, you may have intended to pursue a completely different career but an unexpected incident in your life has dramatically changed your mind. It has to be said that this dramatic event must have occurred very recently otherwise you would have had time to obtain the necessary experience expected of you.

- If you have not had any work experience, for whatever reason, can you demonstrate enthusiasm by your activities elsewhere? In many caring roles, for instance, you could not be employed until you were qualified, but you might well be able to gain experience through voluntary work. Your hobbies, leisure interests or additional study in your free time can also demonstrate your enthusiasm—provided they are relevant.

At this point, look through all your answers and ask if they give a good impression of your determination and drive. Do you feel there is anything lacking on unconvincing about them? If so, perhaps you should stop and ask yourself where you are going in life—and why. If you can't convince *yourself* that you have a good reason for doing something, you are unlikely to be able to convince anyone else.

GETTING YOUR ACT TOGETHER

Have all your pre-interview preparations completed the day before, just as you would for a job interview:

- Check your travelling schedule.
- Have your interview outfit ready to wear.
- Organise what you will need to take with you.
- Know who to contact at the college in an emergency.

Re-read the section in chapter 4 which deals with this stage of your preparation in greater detail.

ATTENDING THE COLLEGE INTERVIEW

College interviews are usually less formal than job interviews. Where the student is under eighteen, parents may also be invited to attend to look round the college at the same time. In some cases they may be asked to be present during the interview, though not to take part.

The interview is usually on a one-to-one basis, the interviewer most likely to be the senior tutor involved in the course. There are occasions, however, when the college principal may also be present, or a second tutor. So the same rule applies as for job interviews—*be prepared for anything.*

Not including an entrance examination or test, the interview itself will typically last 30–45 minutes and concentrate on the following:

- Your family background.
- Your educational achievements.
- Your reasons for choosing a particular career.
- Why the course appealed to you above any alternative there might have been.
- Why you chose to apply to this college in preference to any other offering similar courses.
- How you occupy yourself outside school hours.
- What work experience or hobbies you have that demonstrate your motivation to pursue your career.

At the end of the interview, you will be invited to ask questions, so do take the opportunity of clarifying any points you may have on your list of queries which have not been answered during the course of the interview.

Dos and don'ts of college interviews

Do:
Remember to present yourself in a positive light.
Listen carefully to the questions you are asked.
Answer the question asked and not the question you would have liked to have been asked.
Answer all the questions honestly.
Consciously try to relax.
Treat any examination or test as an important part of the interview process.

Don't:
Reduce your answers to a simple 'yes' or 'no' if more information is required.
Behave in a casual, off-hand or pompous manner.
Smoke.
Swear.
Drink alcohol or take stimulants or relaxants before the interview.

Good luck!

CHECKLIST

1. Can you attend at the time and date specified or do you need to make alternative arrangements?

2. Have you planned your travelling schedule to allow sufficient time for your journey?

3. Do you know what you are expected to take with you?

4. Will there be any sort of test or examination as part of the interview?

5. Do you know exactly what this test or examination involves?

6. If you fail the test or examination, will this prevent you from being selected?

7. Does any of the information you have received from the college need clarifying?

8. Are there any aspects of your personal presentation which need to be brushed up before the interview?

9. Are you quite clear why you have chosen the course?

10. Are you quite clear why you have chosen the college?

11. How will you be able to show you have the skills and abilities to successfuly complete the course?

11

Getting Started on Your Own

GOING IT ALONE

Being your own boss is an attractive idea, but setting up in business on your own is not an easy option. It takes hard work to achieve success.

Self-employment involves long hours and demands total commitment, particularly in the first few years until your business is well established. Even then, you can't afford to stand still in a competitive world. You need to find new outlets or new ideas to match the changes in the market demand. There's essential paperwork to be dealt with, financial planning, rigorous book-keeping and active marketing.

Having a good idea is only the beginning. You also have to find ways of developing, financing and selling it. Will your product or service be marketable? Will there be a regular demand for what you have to offer? Are there any competitors, and if so how can you market your product or service to make it that little bit different?

It isn't just your product or service that has to 'sell' either. First of all you have to be confident that you can 'sell' yourself, to financial backers, potential customers and the wider 'audience' of people who as yet do not realise they cannot live without an automatic goldfish feeder, or a house-sitting service.

LOOKING FOR ADVICE

Where can I get basic information?

You will not be short of sound business advice if you know where to look for it. Useful guidance can be obtained from:

- **Training and Enterprise Councils** (TECs) or **Local Enterprise Companies** (in Scotland). Your local TEC will be listed in the telephone directory or can be contacted through any Jobcentre.

- **Chambers of Trade**. Consulting the local group in the area you work in can be a useful way of discovering potential openings for your business. The secretary's name, address and phone number can usually be found at branch libraries. If you draw a blank there, contact the nearest district office of the **Chamber of Commerce, Trade and Industry** listed in the phone book.

* **Business Link.** This is a Department of Trade and Industry initiative in England run by private sector partnerships of TECs, chambers of commerce, enterprise agencies, local authorities, Government and other providers of business support. Although more focused on existing businesses, those wanting to start new business ventures also have access to available resources and information. To find out what is available in your area phone the national Business Link number 0345 567 765. Your call will be charged at a local rate. In Scotland you need to contact the **Scottish Business Shop Network** on 0800 78 78 78. In Wales your contact point is **Business Connect** on 0345 96 97 98 and if you live in Ulster, the **Local Enterprise Development Unit Small Business Agency** on (01232) 491031.

* **Local initiatives**. These can usually be found in your local telephone directory listed under **Enterprise Agencies**.

FINANCING YOUR PROJECT

For many young people this is often the major stumbling block. There are several ways of tackling it. Possible options include:

* bank loans or overdrafts—if you are over 18
* loans or gifts from relatives or friends
* DTI initiatives run by local TECs or LECs.
* loans or grants from nationally organised enterprise schemes
* grants from company sponsored or local authority initiatives.

Going to the Bank

Don't panic. Seeing the bank manager is not the first step. All the major banks provide useful and comprehensive information packs for small or start-up businesses, which not only provide details of what the bank can offer in the way of services to a would-be entrepreneur, but also basic, sound advice on what you need to do, and know, before taking the plunge.

Constraints on banks when lending money

Even if you have a first class idea, and are confident you have tested the market and found a gap that needs filling, both legal requirements and 'good banking practice' may prevent you from being eligible for a loan. Here are two reasons why:

1. Banks cannot lend money to a minor (anyone under the age of 18). This is illegal.

2. Banks are businesses themselves, not charities. They could not exist if they kept losing money. Consequently, they have to operate within certain guidelines, and most of these present major problems for young entrepreneurs.

Sharing the risk
To begin with, banks do not normally lend money without you making a contribution of around 50% towards the projected cost of the venture—putting your money where your mouth is, if you like. Very often young people do not have sufficient savings to meet this requirement.

Security for loans
Banks also like to be certain that if the business fails, there is some security (a house or stock market shares, for instance) which you could sell to pay off what you owe them. A young person is unlikely to have either of these resources.

Track record
The most difficult hurdle to cross, however, even if you have sufficient financial backing, is lack of experience. Your business skills, and determination to succeed through thick and thin, are as yet untried—which means lending you money is a risky business.

First steps to a business plan
This is not to say that the high street banks won't help. They are more than willing to provide advice and guidance, particularly with the possibly daunting task of drawing up a Business Plan. After all, you may well become a future customer if you aren't one already.

Make an appointment at the bank of your choice—there is usually a member of staff (not necessarily the manager) who is specially trained to deal with small business enquiries—and talk through your proposition. Make sure before you get this far that you have read through all the bank's literature very thoroughly so that you know what sort of questions you are likely to be asked—and can answer them.

Financial aid from friends or relatives

Family and friends can be a valuable source of financial help in the early days. But don't take this sort of generosity for granted; be certain you understand the basis on which money is given or loaned to you. How long is the loan for? What interest or share of profits will be due to the lender? Preferably have the arrangement put in writing and agreed by both of you so that no misunderstandings can arise in the future which could sour relationships.

Department of Trade and Industry initiatives

Unlike the **Prince's Youth Business Trust** and *Live*WIRE, which are set up specifically for the young entrepreneur (see below), DTI initiatives are aimed at the wider business community.

Government supported schemes to help businesses have a habit of coming and going with alarming frequency, or varying in the way they operate from area to area, sometimes because of European funding requirements.

In England, **Business Link** operates through local delivery companies which meet standards of service laid down by the DTI. In the past the growing number of business information sources was becoming counterproductive, confusing instead of helping the business community. **Business Link** has been set up to overcome this: it works as a one-stop shop offering a wide range of services, such as advice on finance, planning, marketing, technology and database information as well as specific funding assistance available in your area. **Business Link** also organises events such as seminars, workshops and conferences on business-related topics and provides **business advisers** who have specialist skills covering all aspects of business life. These independent consultants have been selected for their ability to identify business problems and to come up with the most appropriate solutions.

In Scotland, **Local Enterprise Companies**, in conjunction with other interested parties such as local authorities and chambers of trade, operate **Business Shops**. The concept is the same as **Business Link** in England with a very positive attitude towards the younger entrepreneur. The same applies in Wales, where **Business Connect** has a Start-Up programme which encourages young people starting their own businesses. In Northern Ireland, the **Small Business Agency** of the **Local Enterprise Development Unit** provides similar help.

The Prince's Youth Business Trust (PYBT)

Formed in 1986 through the involvement of the Prince of Wales, as its title suggests, this charitable trust is aimed at helping the young entrepreneur get a foothold on the business ladder. It offers finance, professional advice, training and marketing opportunities. It is particularly interested in helping those who, through no fault of their own, have not had the advantages that many other people of the same age may take for granted.

Qualifying conditions
You can apply to the PYBT for assistance if:

- you are between 18 and 30 years of age;
- you are unemployed;
- you have a viable, imaginative business idea; and
- you cannot get your business off the ground without support for some or all of your finance which cannot be raised elsewhere.

Grants and help
The PYBT can provide a grant of up to £1,500 for tools, equipment, transport, fees, insurance and training, and low interest loans up to £5,000 for stock, equipment or working capital.

Additionally, there are Test Marketing Grants of up to £250 before you start trading to help with the cost of market research and the preparation of a business plan.

Support and practical help are also provided through a personal **business adviser** who acts as a counsellor once your business starts trading. The adviser is a volunteer who will be able to provide you with appropriate business advice whenever you need it. There is also marketing support for your business on an individual or group basis with opportunities to participate in exhibitions as a way of helping you sell your products or services. The PYBT will be able to advise you on what business training opportunities exist in your area.

The Trust operates in England, Wales and Northern Ireland on a regional basis with Area Managers available to discuss your proposal and advise whether or not a PYBT grant or loan is the best way to finance your business. Details of your nearest Area Manager are available in the telephone directory.

The **Prince's Scottish Youth Business Trust** (PSYBT) which operates north of the Border was formed in 1988. It is an independent Scottish company limited by guarantee with charitable status, and has slightly different qualifying conditions to its PYBT counterpart. The age range is 18–25 years (or 30 if you have a disability) and it is not necessary to be unemployed to receive their help. The PSYBT are interested in young people who wish to make the move from employment to self-employment but need support and financial assistance to do so. Ideas must be viable, but don't need to be imaginative. The PSYBT are just as enthusiastic about a would-be painter and decorator as an Internet café. Grant aid, however, is limited to £1,000 only and there are no Test Marketing Grants available. The Trust operates through a network of Regional Managers and details of your nearest manager are available in the telephone directory.

Funding from both the PYBT and PSYBT will depend not only on your enthusiasm and a strong determination to succeed, but also on your ability to provide solid evidence of in-depth planning and research, and your willingness to accept business counselling and training.

*Live*WIRE

*Live*WIRE was set up in 1982 and is supported nationally by Shell UK Ltd and on a local basis by over two hundred other private and public sector organisations. The purpose of *Live*WIRE is to develop and manage good quality programmes which help young people between the ages of 16 and 30 to create and develop their own business enterprises.

Operating throughout the UK, *Live*WIRE has developed a network of co-ordinators and voluntary **business advisers** who provide support and guidance to young people exploring and developing their business ideas, including help with writing up a business plan stating how and why your business will work.

*Live*WIRE programmes on offer include:

LiveWIRE Outreach Programme
This programme raises awareness of self-employment as a challenging but realistic and achievable option for young people. There is a free interactive booklet available entitled *Could This Be You?* which aims to help with the process of thinking through what is involved in starting and running a business. Those who want to pursue the possibility further can be linked with a local **business adviser** who can help with the development of ideas and begin planning the business. Enquirers can also request a 'Business Opportunity Profile' factsheet explaining what is involved in setting up a specific business idea.

LiveWIRE Business Planning Process
This encourages sound business planning and monitoring on a continual basis and helps young entrepreneurs to be more flexible and responsive to opportunities which arise which often improve profitability.

LiveWIRE Business Start Up Awards
This prestigious annual competition provides over £200,000 of cash and 'in kind' support to recognise the nation's most promising young business people in their first year of trading. Over 80 awards presentations take place each year at county, regional and national levels, leading to the *Live*WIRE UK Final. To enter the competition you need to have produced a good business plan and be aged under 26 on the competition closing date.

LiveWIRE Business Growth Challenge
This is designed to help the young owner manager of a small business to develop the skills necessary to manage a growing business.

LiveWIRE Export Challenge
Backed by Shell with additional support and funding from Bass plc, Holiday Inns and Air UK, this programme provides specialist export training and advice, including organised trade visits to Europe and is designed to help businesses to develop an export strategy and gain a foothold in overseas markets.

LiveWIRE International
Following the success of *Live*WIRE in the UK, similar schemes have been set up in Australia, Chile, Colombia, the Bahamas, Hungary, Oman, South Africa and Zambia.

*Live*WIRE has also achieved the International Quality Standard ISO9001. It you want to know more and you are aged between 16 and 30, contact the national *Live*WIRE hotline 0345 573252. Your call will be charged at the local rate. If you prefer to write, their address is:

*Live*WIRE
Hawthorn House, Forth Banks
Newcastle upon Tyne NE1 3SG
Tel: (0191) 261 5584. Fax: (0191) 261 1910
E-Mail: livewire@project.ne.co.uk

Local and regional initiatives

There are many business initiatives throughout the UK which operate on a local or regional basis. Some local authorities and businesses offer funding packages for start-up purposes. Details of what might be available in your area should be found at your local Jobcentre, **Enterprise Agency** or by contacting the local authority.

HANDLING AN INTERVIEW WITH A BUSINESS ADVISER

Prince's Youth Business Trust and *Live*WIRE advisers are specially trained in counselling young people who come to them with business ideas. They are an ideal testing ground for you to learn how to approach other financial backers in future. They understand that you are very new at the game and will need more support and guidance than someone who is much older. He or she will be a good listener and will be prepared to give your idea, however wild, a fair hearing.

Your first meeting will be an informal discussion to look at the basic viability of your proposal, and to agree an action plan for the coming months with specific targets to aim for during that period, such as completing your market survey, finding premises, or working out a sales strategy.

MAKING THE MOST OF YOUR FIRST COUNSELLING SESSION

Background work

It's the old, old story—*be prepared.* A counselling session is just like a job interview in this respect, so do treat it as such. You may be new at the business game, but you want to show that you have a basic grasp of what is expected.

Buy a day-a-page diary
Don't go mad. Buy one which is not too large and bulky—just sufficient to record appointments, names, addresses and telephone numbers, and any other notes you may want to make if you are out and about. Expensive personal organisers at this stage are not necessary.

Buy a robust A4 ring binder and note pad
The PVC covered ones usually last longer and stand up to wear and tear.

Write up your business idea

Show what research you have done to prove there is a demand for your product or service, or a gap in the market which your product or service will fill. This can be a difficult task without some professional help. Don't worry too much. As long as you can prove you have completed at least some basic research—either by notes of a survey carried out in the High Street or newspaper cuttings showing lists of services on offer over a period of time in your local paper—your counsellor will suggest other methods of market research to help you back up your case.

Identify how your product or service will differ from close competitors

If it doesn't, show how you intend to market it from another angle to make it more appealing. Keep your notes brief so they can easily be picked out during discussion sessions.

Identify your potential customers

Who is going to want what you have to offer? What evidence have you that there are going to be enough customers to make the business thrive in your locality? Will you have to operate over a wider area—and how will this affect the way you run the business? Will you need transport for deliveries? Will you need someone to work for you straightaway? What will this involve? And so on.

Plans for getting started

If you aren't clear in your mind as to the scale of your operations, you will not be able to draw up a comprehensive list of everything you need to get started, which is the next job on your list.

What will you need to set up the business?
eg premises
    vehicles
    office furniture
    office equipment
    plant and machinery
    tools
    finance.

What will you need to keep going?
eg raw materials
    suppliers
    outlets

bridging finance between delivery of product/service and payment from customer.

What additional training do you need?
eg book-keeping
marketing
keyboard skills
computing
assertiveness.

The above list is not exhaustive. It is meant only to act as a trigger to help you put together as comprehensive a list as possible. The more detailed your groundwork, the easier it will be for your counsellor to help you.

An example to work on
Even the simplest business demands planning. To show just how much, and to get your mind working along the right lines, go through all the above stages for setting up in business as a window cleaner in a suburban area with a wide range of architecture from Georgian mansions to present day town housing. Then ask yourself what additional requirements would be needed if you expanded the business to include the neighbouring area which has a high proportion of shops and offices. You might be surprised at how much preparation and planning is involved.

Looking the part
Counsellors will not penalise you for turning up for your discussion in a T-shirt and jeans *but* the business of being in business means first and foremost *selling yourself* to financial backers and to potential customers.

Give some thought to how you should dress for different occasions. What is the message you want to get across? When you make business calls, are you projecting the image that is the right one? Remember—judgements will be made about you during those vital first few minutes and the wrong impression can be difficult to overcome once it is firmly established.

The safest course of action is to look in the mirror and see yourself from the point of view of the person you are meeting. You want to match their expectations of you. If a business adviser or potential customer meets you on your home ground—in your workshop for instance, then you have every right to be dressed in your overalls up to your elbows in grease. But if you are meeting them in their own environment it may be less appropriate, particularly if the meeting is to take place in an office rather than on the shop floor. Meeting financial backers does not necessarily mean donning a pin stripe suit, but smart casual wear would be preferable to everyday work clothes.

Attending the interview—things to do

Keep to the time set for the appointment
Remember, business advisers are volunteers. Neither they nor their company are paid for spending time with you. If you have problems keeping your appointment, always contact your adviser to keep him or her in the picture.

Take your work notes with you
These show you have thought through your ideas beyond the stage of being nothing more than a vague series of possibilities.

Take the opportunity to talk openly about your proposal
Your adviser will get a better picture of what you are aiming to achieve and be able to gauge your enthusiasm and commitment.

Be prepared to take any advice offered
If you go into your interview with predetermined notions, or an unwillingness to carry out certain basic work because it all seems too boring, you will be wasting everyone's time. Your adviser has the experience to know what makes the difference between the venture which staggers from crisis to crisis, and one which is set to grow and flourish.

Make every effort to meet the targets which you agree with your adviser
They are a vital part of your action plan. The targets will be realistic ones, possibly very simple in the first instance, but once again, they represent the basic building blocks of getting a business onto a firm footing right from the start.

Attending the interview—things not to do

Don't worry if your adviser asks you a question you can't answer straight away
Note down what you need to find out and ask how you can find the

information if you don't know where to begin. The great difference between an interview with a business counsellor and a recruiter is that you are involved in an exchange of ideas rather than an interrogation. So don't clam up. Your adviser may not realise you have no idea how to go about finding the answers you need.

Don't expect to come away with a fat start-up cheque at the end of the first session
No one is going to throw money at you until you have proved you have a workable idea.

Don't underestimate the time or effort involved
in setting up a business on a proper footing. Don't try to run before you can walk.

Don't be disheartened
if your original idea suddenly does not look so promising. A slightly different approach to marketing may be all that is needed—but expect your adviser to be frank with you if you genuinely cannot hope to succeed.

Thousands of young people are being helped financially every year to set up in their own businesses. With an original idea, sound planning and hard work, you could very well be one of them.

CHECKLIST
1. Have you the real commitment, enthusiasm and motivation to be self-employed?
2. How do you plan to convey this to a business counsellor?
3. What exactly is your business proposal?
4. What market are you aiming for?
5. What demand is there for your product or service?
6. What makes your idea different from your competitors?
7. What will you need to set up your business?
8. What will you need to keep it going?
9. Who should you approach for help?
10. Have you prepared your case well enough to make the best use of your first counselling session?
11. Are you genuinely prepared to take advice when offered and to act on it?
12. Are you prepared if necessary to scrap your original plan and start from scratch, approaching your idea from a different angle?

Useful Addresses

Institute of Personnel and Development, IPD House, Camp Road, Wimbledon, London SW19 4UX. Tel: (0181) 971 9000. Fax: (0181) 263 3333. E-mail: ipd@pd.co.uk Web site: www.ipd.co.uk

The Commission for Racial Equality, Elliot House, 10–12 Allington Street, London SW1E 5EH. Tel: (0171) 828 7022. E-mail: info@cre.gov.uk Web site: www.cre.gov.uk

The Equal Opportunities Commission, Overseas House, Quay Street, Manchester M3 3HN. Tel: (0161) 833 9244. E-mail: info@eoc.org.uk Web site: www.eoc.org.uk

The Northern Ireland Labour Relations Agency, 2/8 Gordon Street, Belfast BT1 2LG. Tel: (01232) 321442. Fax: (01232) 330827. E-mail: lra@dnet.co.uk Web site: www.lra.org.uk

Local Enterprise Development Unit Small Business Agency, Upper Galwally, Belfast 8. Tel: (01232) 491031. Fax: (01232) 691432. E-mail: ledu@ledu-ni.gov.uk Web site: www.ledu-ni.gov.uk

The British Psychological Society, St Andrews House, 48 Princess Road East, Leicester LE1 7DR. Tel: (0116) 254 9568. Fax: (0116) 247 0787. E-mail: mail@bps.org.uk Web site: www.bps.org.uk

The Prince's Scottish Youth Business Trust, Mercantile Chambers, 6th Floor, 53 Bothwell Street, Glasgow G2 6TS. Tel: (0141) 248 4999. Fax: (0141) 248 4836.

Career Analysts Ltd, Career House, 90 Gloucester Place, London W1H 4BL. Tel: (0171) 935 5452. Fax: (0171) 486 9922.

*Live*WIRE, Hawthorn House, Forth Banks, Newcastle-upon-Tyne, NE1 3SG. Tel: (0191) 261 5584. Fax: (0191) 261 1910. E-Mail: livewire@project.ne.co.uk Web site: www.shell-livewire.org

Further Reading

Body language: How to read others' thoughts by their gestures, Alan Pease (Sheldon Press)
Code of Practice for the elimination of racial discrimination and the promotion of equality of opportunity in employment (Commission for Racial Equality)
Fair and Efficient Selection (Equal Opportunities Commission)
How to be an Entrepreneur: A Guide for the Under 25s, Ian Phillipson (Kogan Page)
How to Communicate at Work, Ann Dobson (How To Books)
How to Get That Job, Joan Fletcher (How To Books)
How to Know Your Rights at Work, Robert Spicer (How To Books). Covers the legal rights of job applicants as well as employees.
How to Manage Your Career, Roger Jones (How To Books)
How to Market Yourself, Ian Phillipson (How To Books)
How to Pass Selection Tests, Mike Bryon and Sanjay Modha (Kogan Page)
How to Pass Technincal Selection Tests, Mike Bryon and Sanjay Modha (Kogan Page)
How to Pass Verbal Reasoning Tests, Harry Tolley and Ken Thomas (Kogan Page)
How to Pass Numeracy Tests, Harry Tolley and Ken Thomas (Kogan Page)
How to Survive at College, David Acres (How To Books)
Interviews: How to Succeed, Judy Skeats (Ward Lock)
The Job Book: Training and Career Choices for School and College Leavers (Hobsons Press)
The Kompass Register
Mastering Public Speaking, Anne Nicholls (How To Books)
Starting a Business from Home, Graham Jones (How To Books)
Who Owns Whom (Dun and Bradstreet)

Glossary

accredited user: someone qualified to adminster psychometric tests.

Advisory, Conciliation and Arbitration Service (ACAS): an independent and impartial body providing free information and advice, working to prevent or resolve industrial disputes, and the promotion of good practice and harmonious relationships in the workplace.

aptitude tests: a series of exercises to be completed within a given time to show whether or not you have the skills or abilities needed to be proficient at a particular job.

body language: the conscious or unconscious signals given to others by using certain gestures, facial expressions and body movements.

British Psychological Society (BPS): the professional body for practising psychologists in Great Britain.

Business Connect: one-stop shop advice service for businesses in Wales.

business counsellor (or adviser): a successful businessman or woman who gives basic advice and guidance on how to set up in business on your own.

Business Link: A Department of Trade and Industry initiative designed as a one-stop shop for advice services operating through local delivery companies in England.

business plan: a detailed analysis of what product or service you want to sell, how you intend to sell it, what finance, premises and machinery you will need and what your short- and long-term objectives are.

Business Shop: a Scottish Office initiative operating through LECs to provide advice and guidance to businesses in Scotland.

career history: the record of your working life comprising job descriptions, main duties and responsibilities, names and addresses of employers and dates when employed.

Chamber of Trade: a group of businessmen and women who work together to promote local trade.

closed questions: fact-finding questions which restrict answers to 'Yes' or 'No'.

cloven-hoof effect: the reduction of your chances of success arising from a single aspect of your appearance or behaviour causing disapproval. See also **halo effect**.

Commission for Racial Equality (CRE): an organisation set up under the Race Relations Act 1976 to work towards the elimination of discrimination and to promote good relations between different racial groups.

competencies: a range of skills or abilities necessary to meet standards which have been identified as essential for the good performance of a job.

conditions of employment: the terms on which a particular job is offered by an employer.

contract of employment: the legally binding agreement made between an employer and employee to confirm acceptance on both sides of the **conditions of employment**.

Customer Services Department: the department of an organisation which deals directly with the public to resolve customer difficulties or queries.

Enterprise Agency: an information and counselling service jointly funded by the **public** and **private sector** to help develop new and expanding small businesses and to improve employment opportunities in local communities.

Equal Opportunities Commission (EOC): an organisation set up under the Sex Discrimination Act 1975 to promote equality of opportunity between the sexes.

eye contact: a means of maintaining good communication with someone during an interview or conversation by moving the area of concentration within the triangle formed by the other person's eyes and the end of their nose.

group culture: an agreed set of 'rules' or attitudes adopted by a group of people with which only members of the group can identify.

halo effect: the enhancement of your chances of success brought about by a single aspect of your appearance or behaviour meeting with approval. See also **cloven hoof effect**.

in-house candidate: a candidate for a job vacancy who is already employed by the organisation in which the vacancy occurs.

Institute of Personnel and Development (IPD): the professional organisation for those working in personnel, training and development (human resources) in the UK and the Republic of Ireland.

interpersonal chemistry: the instinctive reaction of one person to another when meeting for the first time.

interpersonal skills: your ability to relate to or react with other people in social or working environments.

job description: a list of broadly defined duties and responsibilities attached to a particular job.

job title: the name given to a particular job by an employing organisation.

key word: a word which acts as a memory jogger to a series of interrelated topics.

Kompass Register: a work of reference in four volumes listing around 30,000 UK companies, their products and services, financial performance, number of employees, sales offices and so on.

line manager: a manager responsible for the operational or production processes of a company.

***Live*WIRE:** a scheme primarily sponsored by Shell UK to develop and manage programmes which improve opportunities for young people to create and develop new businesses.

Local Enterprise Development Unit Small Business Agency: a service available to small businesses in Northern Ireland.

motivational drives: aspects of personality which make one decide to do one thing rather than another.

Murphy's Law: the supposition that what can go wrong will go wrong.

occupational psychologist: a trained practitioner in human behaviour who can advise through the use of psychometric tests on the best career to match individual skills, personality and **motivational drives**.

open questions: questions which give an opportunity to provide a full answer including explanations or additional information as necessary.

organisational structure: how a business or organisation is divided up into divisions, departments and so on for the purposes of production processes or managerial control.

panel interview: an interview with more than three interviewers sitting together, usually acting under the guidance of a chairman or woman. (Panel interviews tend to be used for senior appointments, particularly in the **public sector**.)

personality questionnaire: a questionnaire designed to identify a person's **personality traits** used by employers to help match the right person to the demands of a job.

personality traits: a set of characteristics which can be grouped together to forecast a person's response to particular situations.

Prince's Scottish Youth Business Trust (PSYBT): an independent Scottish company limited by guarantee with charitable status set up to provide financial help and support to young people in Scotland wishing to set up their own business.

Prince's Youth Business Trust (PYBT): a charitable trust set up to provide financial backing and professional advice to young people, particularly those who are disadvantaged, who are setting up or already running their own businesses.

private sector: that part of the country's economy which is owned and operated by private individuals and firms.

psychometric tests: aptitude tests and psychometric questionnaires designed to measure a range of skills, general intelligence, **personality traits** and **motivational drives**.

Public Relations Department: the department of an organisation with responsibility for providing members of the public with the best possible image of the organisation concerned.

public sector: that part of the economy which includes government financed industry and the social services including the health service, government departments and local government.

short list: the small number of candidates selected from the larger number of applicants to attend for interview.

Training and Enterprise Councils (TECs) (or Local Enterprise Companies in Scotland): government funded agencies run by local industrialists and other employers who are responsible for co-ordinating government training and enterprise projects locally.

transferable skills: special talents or abilities which can be adapted or reshaped by an individual to suit different working environments.

Travel to Interview Scheme: a scheme operated by the Employment Service to help unemployed people meet travelling expenses when attending interviews at a distance.

Who Owns Whom: a work of reference published by Dun and Bradstreet detailing UK company ownership, and connections.

work experience: the time you spend in a working environment acquiring skills and knowledge of working practices.

Index